A Cookbook:
Helpful Cooking Hints for HouseHusbands of Uppity Women

E-Heart Press, Inc.
3700 Mockingbird Lane
Dallas, Texas 75205

Please send me _____ copies of **A Cookbook: Helpful Cooking Hints for HouseHusbands of Uppity Women** $12.95

Postage/Handling for 1 book $1.75

Add .50 for each additional book   _____

Texas residents add 8% sales tax   _____

TOTAL   _____

Send to: _____

Address _____

City _____ State _____ Zip _____

Make checks payable to E-Heart Press, Inc.

- -

A Cookbook:
Helpful Cooking Hints for HouseHusbands of Uppity Women

E-Heart Press, Inc.
3700 Mockingbird Lane
Dallas, Texas 75205

Please send me _____ copies of **A Cookbook: Helpful Cooking Hints for HouseHusbands of Uppity Women** $12.95

Postage/Handling for 1 book $1.75

Add .50 for each additional book   _____

Texas residents add 8% sales tax   _____

TOTAL   _____

Send to: _____

Address _____

City _____ State _____ Zip _____

Make checks payable to E-Heart Press, Inc.

A Cookbook:

Helpful Cooking Hints
for
HouseHusbands
of
Uppity Women

A Cookbook:

Helpful Cooking Hints
for
HouseHusbands
of
Uppity Women

by

Archie P. McDonald

1988 E-Heart Press, Inc. Dallas, Texas

Library of Congress Cataloging-in-Publication Data

McDonald, Archie P.
    A Cookbook: Helpful cooking hints for househusbands
of uppity women by Archie P. McDonald.
        p.   cm.
    Includes index.
    ISBN 0-935014-11-X
    1. Cookery, I. Title.
TX652.M364 1988
    641.5— dc19   87-17781
                                                        CIP

First published in 1988 by:
E-Heart Press, Inc.
3700 Mockingbird Lane
Dallas, Texas 75205

Design and type by:
O-Tree-O Creations
Austin, Texas

DEDICATED TO

JUDY

The world's most Classic, Grade A,

Number One, All-Time, All-American

Uppity Woman,

and all the rest of

her kind.

The Making of a HouseHusband

It all started, appropriately, by the dawn's early light. Eve prepared the first meal for Adam by serving him a forbidden apple. Husbands have been snake-bitten ever since when it comes to getting food on the table. For ages after Adam enjoyed that first forbidden meal, men toiled to provide their bread, women baked it, and the family shared the result of their joint labors. Things began to change.

In the middle of the nineteenth century feminists such as Susan B. Anthony and Amelia Bloomer spread the new gospel that women had rights, among them the prerogative to vote, wear funny clothes, and avoid the kitchen. In other words, they became Uppity. Then was born the New Man, the *homo sapius domesticus*, or, as he is better known in modern society, the HouseHusband.

Some HouseHusbands sew and wash and iron clothes. Women dropped ironing like a hot potato when wash-and-wear was invented. Some HouseHusbands run the vacuum cleaner, change the baby's diapers, and do anything else required to keep the household going. It is not my intention to help you learn to do any of these things. Sewing machines are self-willed mechanical beasts best avoided. I recommend that you establish an intimate relationship with the alterations person at your nearest dry cleaning establishment. Washing machines are operated easily and come with clear instructions. Irons are no more fun for you than they were for your mate. Ditto vacuum cleaners. Anyone can plug one in, turn on the switch, and aim the noisy thing at the dirt. Diapers are disgusting and should not be discussed by sensitive people in person, much less in print.

What I hope this book *will* do is help you learn to feed your kids, yourself, and even your Uppity Woman if you feel charitable. Your may agree with the character in Leon Hale's *Turn South at the Second Bridge*, who observed that ". . .the light bread people is ruinin' our women. . .," but pouting about it will not warm your belly.

The Revolution began at our house after twenty years of marriage. We said our vows in 1957 whilst in college, I in my senior year and she in the sophomore year. We set up housekeeping in a rented apartment. Except for each other our most entertaining diversion was to turn on a light in the middle of the night to watch the cockroaches scamper for cover. I finished college while she worked to support us. Then an offer came to work on an advanced degree, so I did that and she worked and supported us. Then an offer came to work on an even more advanced degree, so I did that and she worked and supported us.

The life of a gigolo was good. I did the thing I did best — go to school — and she did everything else. She earned our money, kept the house, and did the shopping. Best of all, she cooked superbly in the Southern, especially East Texas Southern, style. She had learned to do so while still in high school after her mother went to work. I should have realized when I learned this that history would repeat itself; it was either genetic or prophetic. But blinded by young love and dulled by a full belly, I assumed the good life would last forever.

Then came the babies. She had to stay home and I had to go to work. That wasn't too much of an adjustment because I had pursued a course of study that kept me in school on the other side of the teacher's desk. She stayed at home now and could cook all the more. I even got to go home to lunch.

Years passed. Cub Scouts, the Women's Faculty Club, and PTA and a dozen more organizations recruited my cook to pursue their endless tampering with society and the good life. More and more dinners became warmed-up leftovers and "quick" meals. Worst of all, we "ate out" where they concocted even "quicker" meals.

Then, one fateful day, a person I had always thought to be my friend called to say he needed a half-time secretary. Would she be interested? Could the various organizations she now served as president spare her half of each day? They could. At least they agreed to employ her in the evenings, usually around suppertime.

Then she remembered that she had interrupted her own education to finance mine, so she went back to finish her baccalaureate degree. Naturally she made the Dean's Honor Roll with straight "A" grades until she was graduated, something that had eluded me for nine years of college. Then several people, even several whom I also had regarded previously as friends, convinced her that the City Fathers needed a City Mother to help them run the town. Of course she won the election.

Then a financial institution decided that she would be their best bet to help them move into the 1980s in their marketing program. They put her on the radio and the television doing commercials and in charge of this and that and the other.

8

Then the Governor of the Sovereign State of Texas put her on two committees. The state Land Commissioner and the state Treasurer did the same, and her state professional trade association came up with a few duties and. . . . Most of all, there came a time when the Lord Mayor of our town, a man who had held the position for thirteen years, decided to call it quits. And who, do you suppose, did he feel was the appropriate person in the city government to succeed him? Was it the car dealer, or the assistant school superintendent, or the oil field land man, all good men and true? Of course not! We live in the Liberated Age. You can guess what happened. Only the Almighty knows where it is going to end.

One thing we do know is that all this has wrought major changes in our household. Behold now the HouseHusband, the unnatural by-product of the making of an Uppity Woman.

To quote Abraham Lincoln, our martyred sixteenth president, out of context, "It is altogether fitting and proper that we do this." She supported me emotionally and financially during my gigolo days and kept up the heavy end of that endeavor while I began a career. Then she had the good sense to step out to utilize her talents and gifts in a fully actualized way.

Modern households like ours abound. Many women *have* to work to help support their families. Others do so to keep from going insane from the repetition of household duties. Their husbands still share the problem of getting the cooking done. We might as well admit that some women are just lazy — being Uppity does not necessarily mean that a woman is industrious. Their husbands have the same problem. All of this means that there are a lot of us who, for no greater motivation than simple hunger, have got to move into the kitchen in self-defense.

According to a survey published in the late 1980s, "more than half of the husbands questioned said they were routinely involved in cooking — almost ninety percent said they shopped for groceries."

When we make this momentous move to the kitchen, some of us learn that cooking is fun. We delight, perhaps spitefully, in finding a new recipe that our Uppity Woman hasn't seen. But watch out. She may start to *bring* you recipes. If this occurs, remind her that your presence in the kitchen is a concession on your part. Utilizing her husband's cooking talents is NOT one of her Natural Rights protected by the ERA amendment. It might even be helpful to remind her that the ERA amendment did not

9

pass — yet. No. Far from being a restaurant where she may order from a menu, she is a guest in *your* kitchen and should accept the fare you have prepared.

Another good thing to keep in mind is that you should never sit silently while she tells you a dish needs more salt or should have been cooked longer. Immediately offer to relinquish your duties and return to the good old days when men were men and women were cooks. Certainly you could not return to the past (remember why you took over the kitchen in the first place), but she never really knows whether you mean it or not. She will not, I repeat, *will not* take a chance.

Occasionally she will offer to help empty the dish washer and put away the cooking utensils. This is a subtle way to sabotage you by hiding or misplacing your favorite mixing bowl, frying pan, or spoon. Indulge her. You can rearrange things later and it helps her to feel a little less guilty because you have had to assume her rightful place in the kitchen.

In the modern world it is necessary for both partners to forget stereotyped roles in the home anyway. The chicken does not care which gender seasons it and places it in the oven. The pan could care less who washes it. You need to cooperate. She can be your best cooking teacher (unless she didn't know how in the first place) and your most adoring fan when you get a dish just right. She may even be moved to volunteer to clean up the kitchen. But don't count on it.

So here you have a book of Helpful Hints for House-Husbands of Uppity Women. The book assumes that you can measure, know the difference between a teaspoon and a table-spoon, and can turn on the oven and the burners on the top of the cookstove. And little else.

Helpful Hints contains sections on meats and casseroles, vegetables, salads, and bread, daily menu planning, shopping advice, and much more. Each recipe will list all ingredients in a given dish, followed by easy, step-by-step procedures that will lead you through the mystery of preparing a few dishes. Follow-ing these simple instructions, you can assemble a presentable meal for breakfast, lunch, and dinner (supper).

So, with apron on, let us go forth to feed the family we love. If you are lucky, your Uppity Woman will arrive just in time to sit down and enjoy the results of your work.

Dramatis Personae

Uppity Woman

Homo sapien femaleus uppitus. The girl you married who promised to love, honor, and obey, an implicit pledge to sew, cook, clean, look after kids, wash the car, keep the firewood cut, and scratch your back. These things are now forgotten in the Liberated Phase of Life. Aprons are traded for briefcases and someone else is hired or intimidated to keep the house cleaned and do the cooking. And it's high heels every day, baby.

HouseHusband

Homo sapius domesticus. The Bread Winner and Lord and Master who formerly came home to a meal he did not prepare, who now has been Liberated.

The Kids

They are the same, only bigger, and what they want to know most is, "When's supper?"

11

A Word About Recipes and Products

Most of the recipes come from my wife or her mother, from my mother, or from good friends. Some are from HouseHusbands, but most are from Uppity Women who brought out yellowed, dog-eared recipe collections they had not used in some time. All are gratefully acknowledged: Ms. Emmie Peacock, Ms. Karen Gehring, Ms. Jeannie Attaway, HH. Sidney Abegg, Ms. Hazel Abernethy, Ms. Sylvia Hunt, Ms. Linda Cross, HH. Greg Beil, HH. Fred Tarpley, HH. Max Lale, Ms. Jewel Cates, HH. Valentine J. Belfiglio, Ms. Martha Emmons, Nem Tucker (my own mother!), Bachelor Pat Butler, and Ms. Freida Johnson. If I have omitted anyone, please forgive me.

None of us accept the slightest responsibility for the outcome of any of this. On the other hand, if *your* meal flops, tell your Uppity Woman that you don't belong in the damned kitchen anyway!

Occasionally I have used a brand name of a product. It should be clearly understood that the author is a HouseHusband, not an advertising agent for any particular brand or product. Most of what I use was found in the kitchen when my Uppity Woman moved out. These things work for me in the recipes described, so I have listed them. Other brands will probably work just as well. If you like, try them to see.

Contents

The Making of a HouseHusband _____ 7

Dramatis Personae _____ 11
    Uppity Woman _____ 11
    HouseHusband _____ 11
    The Kids _____ 11

A Word About Recipes and Products _____ 12

Glossary _____ 20
    Stir _____ 20
    Mix _____ 20
    Combine _____ 20
    Pour _____ 20
    Drain _____ 20
    Tender _____ 20
    Parboil _____ 20
    Simmer _____ 20
    Sauté _____ 20
    Chopping _____ 21
    Mince _____ 21
    Cook _____ 21
    Burn _____ 21
    Dinner _____ 21

Equipping the HouseHusband's Kitchen _____ 22
    Electric Appliances
    Toaster _____ 23
    Coffee Pot _____ 24
    Slow Cookers _____ 25
    Juicer _____ 25
    Blender _____ 25
    Food Processor _____ 25
    Electric Knife _____ 26
    Electric Skillet _____ 26
    Electric Popcorn Popper _____ 26

Electric Grill _____ 26
Electric Warming Grill _____ 26
Microwave Oven _____ 27
Hand Operated Kitchen Tools
Knives _____ 27
Cutting Board _____ 28
Spoons _____ 28
Spatula _____ 28
Tongs _____ 28
Can Opener _____ 28
Timer _____ 29
Ladles _____ 29
Potato Peeler _____ 29
Egg Ring _____ 29
Bacon Press _____ 29
Measuring Cups and Spoons _____ 29
Grater _____ 30
Colander _____ 30
Pots and Pans _____ 30
Casserole Dishes _____ 30
Scissors _____ 31
Meat Mallet _____ 31
Apron _____ 31

Shopping _____ **32**

A Word About Fat _____ **34**

Chapter 1: Meats, Main Dishes, & Casseroles __ 37
Beef
A.P.'s Sirloin Special _____ 40
Baked Hash _____ 41
Beef Stew _____ 42
Brunswick Stew, Texas Style _____ 44
Celestial Spaghetti _____ 46
Chicken Fried Steak and Gravy _____ 48
Corn "Willie" _____ 50
Emmie's Ground Beef Casseroles #1, #2, #3 _____ 51
Enchilada Squares _____ 54
Eye of Round Roast _____ 55

Freida's Pepper Beef _____ 56
Goulash _____ 58
Gypsy Rice B. _____ 59
Italian Swiss Steak _____ 60
Leftover Oriental Disguise _____ 61
Linda's Chili _____ 62
Mean Chili _____ 64
Old-Fashioned Meat Loaf _____ 66
Meat Loaf _____ 67
Mexican Casserole _____ 68
Mexican Corn Bread Casserole _____ 70
Pepper Steak _____ 71
Pepper Steak _____ 72
Porcupines _____ 73
Sour Cream Enchilada Casserole _____ 74
Steak and Potato Casserole _____ 76
Steaks Patrick _____ 78
Son of a Gun Stew _____ 80
Stuffed Bell Peppers _____ 81
Veal with Lemon and Butter _____ 82

Chicken
Barbecued Chicken _____ 83
Bride's Chicken _____ 84
Broiled Chicken _____ 85
Chicken a la Can Can _____ 86
Chicken and Spaghetti _____ 87
Chicken Delight _____ 88
Chicken Enchiladas _____ 89
Chicken N' Rice _____ 90
Chicken With Sherry _____ 91
Company Chicken _____ 92
Crispy Baked Chicken _____ 93
Curry Chicken _____ 94
Greek Chicken _____ 95
Hot Chicken Salad _____ 96
Mexican Chicken Casserole _____ 97
Sour Cream Chicken Breasts _____ 98

Pork
Beans and Sausage Dinner _____ 99
Sausage-Bean Chowder _____ 100
Spanish Pork Chops _____ 102

15

Seafood
Baked White Fish _____ 103
Boiled Shrimp _____ 104
Crawfish Etouffée _____ 106
Salmon Patties _____ 107
Venison
Hazel's Venison Roast _____ 108

Chapter 2: Vegetables _____ 109

Potatoes
Potato Pancakes _____ 113
Stuffed Baked Potatoes _____ 114
Sidney's Potatoes _____ 116
Scalloped Potatoes _____ 118
Easy Scalloped Potatoes _____ 119
New Potatoes _____ 120
Prepare Ahead Potato-Cheese Casserole _____ 121
Bourbon Sweet Potatoes _____ 122
Tomatoes
Broiled Tomatoes _____ 123
Baked Tomatoes _____ 124
Okra and Tomatoes _____ 124
Squash
Steamed Squash _____ 126
Country Style Yellow Squash _____ 127
Cherokee Squash Casserole _____ 128
Squash Croquettes _____ 129
Rice
Rice _____ 130
Rice and Mushrooms _____ 131
Party Rice _____ 132
Spanish Rice _____ 133
Broccoli
Broccoli and Rice _____ 134
Broccoli-Rice Casserole _____ 135
Corn
Fresh Corn on the Cob _____ 136
Corn Casserole _____ 137
Buttered Summer Corn _____ 138

More Fresh Vegetables

Garden Fresh Beans _____ 139
Green Bean Casserole _____ 140
Black "Eyes of Texas " Casserole _____ 140
Dried Lima Beans _____ 142
Dried Pinto Beans _____ 143
Fresh Garden Greens _____ 144
Steamed Fresh Broccoli _____ 145
Fresh Vegetable Sauté _____ 146
Asparagus Casserole _____ 147
Creamed Celery Almandine _____ 148
Green Chili Casserole _____ 149
Cheese Grits _____ 150

Chapter 3: Salads _____ 151

Cauliflower Salad _____ 155
Chicken Salad _____ 156
Crab Salad _____ 157
Fried Apples _____ 158
Fruit Salad _____ 159
Mexican Salad _____ 160
Mystery Salad _____ 161
Chris' Potato Salad _____ 162
Potato Salad _____ 163
Sauerkraut Salad _____ 164
Spinach Salad _____ 165

Chapter 4: Breads _____ 167

Hot Cross Bread _____ 170
Mexican Corn Bread _____ 171
Stove Top Corn Bread _____ 172

Chapter 5: Desserts _____ 175

Better Than Sex Cake _____ 178
Buttermilk Chocolate Pudding Cake _____ 179
Dump Cake _____ 180
Martha's Peach Cobbler _____ 181
Mexican Cookies _____ 182
Mom's Sugar Cookies _____ 183

Chapter 6: Breakfast Foods _____ 185
Breakfast Meats
Bacon _____ 188
Ham _____ 189
Sausage _____ 190
Cereals
Dry Cereal _____ 190
Oatmeal _____ 191
Grits _____ 192
Quick Cream of Wheat _____ 192
Breakfast Breads
Toast _____ 194
English Muffin _____ 194
Biscuits _____ 194
Canned Biscuits _____ 195
Biscuits from a Mix _____ 195
Eggs
Fried-Poached _____ 196
Scrambled _____ 197
Sausage and Egg Casserole _____ 198
Omelets _____ 199
Onion Potato Omelet _____ 199
Judy's Omelet _____ 200
Fresh Fruit
Grapefruit _____ 201
Orange Slices _____ 202
Cantaloupe _____ 202
Spreads
Butter, Margarine, Preserves _____ 203
Beverages Other Than Fruit Juice
Ice Water, Milk, Beer _____ 204
Juices _____ 205
Serving Breakfast _____ 206

Chapter 7: Lunch _____ 207
Soups
Chicken-and-Ham Soup _____ 210
Elephant Soup _____ 212
Garden Vegetable Soup _____ 213
Gazpacho _____ 214
Gazpacho Gringo _____ 215

Quick Chicken Soup _____ 216
Onion Wine Soup _____ 217
Potato Soup _____ 218
Sausage Soup _____ 219
Luncheon (or Dinner) Salad
Tossed Salad _____ 220
Sandwiches
Bologna _____ 221
Bacon and Tomato _____ 222
BLT _____ 223
Peanut Butter/Jelly _____ 224
Picnic Pimento Cheese _____ 225
Side Edibles _____ 226
Beverages _____ 226

Chapter 8: Dinner _____ **227**
Bread _____ 231
Soups and Salads _____ 231
Beverages _____ 231
After Dinner Snack _____ 232

**Chapter 9: Sample Menus: Monday Through
Sunday** _____ **233**

Chapter 10: Write Your Own Cookbook _____ **241**

Glossary

Stir

Using a spoon, a spatula, or your fingers, to vigorously agitate the contents of a bowl, can, pot, or other container.

Mix

The same thing only more vigorously.

Combine

Still the same thing only with more restraint.

Pour

Empty the contents of one container into another.

Drain

Put something that has a lot of liquid around or in it into a colander, a sieve-like device with holes in it, that will allow the liquid to go down the drain.

Tender

That moment when a brittle vegetable, such as a carrot or potato, becomes soft.

Parboil

Literally to boil partially. This means to take it out of the water *before* it is tender, and still partially brittle or crunchy. In other words, it is not yet cooked.

Simmer

A low setting on a cooking stove or range that is difficult to locate. Any inexperienced HouseHusband can cook things on "high" to get it over with quicker. Or, fearful of burning it, some cook it on "low" and wonder why the oatmeal is not ready before lunch. Experienced HouseHusbands soon learn that *first* you boil, then go to "low, low," which is close enough to "simmer."

Sauté

French word for frying things, such as onions and peppers, in oil until they wilt. But who would trust the French?

Chopping
Rendering a defenseless pepper or not-so-defenseless onion into a lot of little slivers or chunks.

Mince
Beat the poor thing into smithereens.

Cook
To reduce raw vegetables and meats to a palatable and belly-filling condition by ingenious combinations subjected to controlled degrees of heat for regulated periods of time.

Burn
1. To allow uncontrolled heat for an unregulated period of time to ruin your ingenious combinations of vegetables and meats.

2. What happens to your fingers when you grip a hot pan without first protecting it with a mitten or pad.

Dinner
Animals "feed" or "graze," but HouseHusbands "dine" when they have mastered the art of reducing raw vegetables and meats to a palatable and belly-filling condition by ingenious combinations of vegetables and meats subjected to controlled degrees of heat for regulated periods of time. And, if an Uppity Woman is present, it is all worthwhile.

Equipping The HouseHusband's Kitchen

Cooking, woodworking, and auto mechanics have at least one thing in common: you have to have the right tools for the job. If you are starting from scratch, this could run into a substantial investment. Unless you are a newlywed, however, this is unlikely to be your circumstance. Before your mate abandoned the kitchen for other worlds to conquer, she probably assembled most of what you will need without your knowing it. If not, take a quick inventory and replace absent necessities.

When you went shopping with her in the past you always abandoned her in the shoe department and spent your time among the hard metal of power tools or the macho, leathery smells of the athletic equipment department. Well, things have changed. For one thing the athletic department is no longer macho. Jane Fonda saw to that. Now they sell, for female jocks, those pastel-colored leg warmers that look so cute and baggy on the lower leg, skimpy and satiny athletic shorts that could pass for lingerie and probably do, and sweat shirts in size Petite, probably pink (yuck!).

More importantly, since you have taken over the cooking, you will have little use for most of the *other* stuff the athletic department sells. Your fishing, bowling, or golfing equipment might as well go in the next (there is always a "next") garage sale.

Now you will spend a lot of your time in the kitchen, so probably you will want to visit the housewares department of your favorite emporium. This may even become your Uppity Woman's source of your next birthday, anniversary, or Valentine's Day gift since you will make absent-minded comments about a new food processor or wok you saw the other day in the store. If this happens, ooh and ah and wow! over such offerings just as if they were shotguns or golf clubs. At least they are not neckties that only a Democrat would wear or those perfumy after shaves she used to produce from the men's department. You know the one that everyone laughed about? It made you smell. . . well, like a lady of the evening. Now you have a FOOD PROCESSOR, boy, and you had better PROCESS.

If you purchase your own tools, you will need certain items for use in your kitchen. Bear in mind that the following are things that I find most useful. Stores are full of gadgets, mostly superfluous to your efforts, but you might want to become a collector of them.

Electric Appliances

Toaster

You can't make toast without a toaster. Toast probably is the first thing you will prepare each morning, so let's start here. There must be at least a hundred brands of the things, but they all perform the same function. With some you just put the bread in the slots and push down the lever to lock the webbing in place until the heat has been on for a regulated amount of time.

Toasting times are communicated on a scale near the lever with words such as "Light" and "Dark." This is not difficult to decipher. Turn the thing one way or the other to obtain your desired degree of "toasting." On most toasters, when their work is done the product will pop up with a resounding metallic click audible in the next room. If you foul up the regulation of the degree of toasting on the first attempt, experiment. You will get the hang of it.

Some companies offer a model that slowly and silently lowers the bread, toasts it, and it then slowly and silently emerges from the bowels of the machine. This can sneak up on you because there is no sound and your toast may be cold before you discover that the beast has fulfilled its singular mission. You can't very well send it down for a warmup, so you might as well start over.

Some toasters, sort of the Cadillac models, feature a little drawer which promises to warm English muffins or danish. It is useful only if you like these things, and I do.

These toaster-ovens will do other things as well. Of course, you will use it mostly to burn white bread, brown brown or whole wheat bread even more, but you can also use the oven to prepare sausages and other meats just as you would in a regular oven. The only limitation is size, and there is good news and bad news: the good news is you will use much less electricity; the bad news, you can't prepare nearly as much because the size of most of these contraptions is about one-twentieth of a regular oven.

I formerly used the old-fashioned pop-up variety of toaster until I gave it an electrical problem with a knife blade (not a recommended implement for retrieving a piece of toast that is stuck). That is how I moved up to a toaster-oven!

Coffee Pot

There are many varieties of coffee pots, and most Uppity Women could care less what kind you choose to brew her morning coffee so long as it is served at the right time and you do not let it get too cold while bringing it to her bed.

Let us agree right now that instant coffee is for sissies. Boiling water and pouring it directly over ground-up flakes and crystals is a poor excuse for a cup of coffee. You can never get it stirred right and for a long time thereafter a brothy film covers the top. Have you ever seen the green things that will grow in the bottom of a cup of instant coffee that sits overnight?

You need a real coffee pot to make real coffee. There are "drip" pots that require you to put the coffee (about a single measure per two cups) into a middle container, pour the right amount of boiling water (surely there is no need to tell even the novice HouseHusband how to boil water!), in relation to the amount of coffee grounds in the middle part, into the top part. Then you just wait for the water to "drip" down through the grounds into the bottom part of the pot. Simple.

Percolators work about the same way. You measure coffee into a container that sits on the top of a stem, put the right amount of (cold) water into the pot, thread the container over the stem, place the stem in its receptacle in the bottom of the pot, and plug the cord into a wall socket. Voilà! Hot coffee in five to ten minutes. Most pots only make about twelve cups, but you can get a thirty-cup pot if your Uppity Woman has to entertain a lot.

THE BEST kind of modern coffee pot is the one that has a little clock in it. You put a filter in a slide-out receptacle, load it with coffee grounds, pour the water into its container, set the clock for about twenty minutes before you plan to rise in the morning, and go to bed. Don't forget to activate the automatic turn-on button or you will be disappointed at 6:00 a.m.

It is impossible for even a novice HouseHusband to become confused with any of this except setting the clock. Check to make sure someone did not unplug the coffeemaker, thus stopping the clock, or that the Friendly Electric Company did not interrupt service, which will also stop the clock. This is important. If you do not get the coffee to the bed on time in the morning the whole day becomes uncertain.

Slow Cookers

Slow cookers, or Crock-Pots, are the HouseHusband's best friend. You can put on some beans, a roast, or a chicken in the morning and your dinner will be well-nigh complete when you return from work in the late afternoon. Again, there are a number of varieties of such pots. They mostly work alike (slowly), and they can be purchased at hardware stores, houseware departments of department stores, and garage sales following the breakup of marriages.

Juicer

A juicer is like a toaster: it does one thing. Since nothing tastes better in the early morning than fresh fruit juice, you have got to have one. They are simple to operate. Plug it in, first attach the spout, then the metal filter (the part with the holes) that lets the juice through but stops the seeds, and the whirligig on top. Cut the oranges or grapefruit in half, press each half down on the whirligig, and squeeze. Be sure to place a glass under the spout first. If you forget, have a wipe rag handy.

Blender

To mere husbands, blenders only do one thing: make frozen daiquiris and margaritas. To HouseHusbands, however, they are a marvel. You can make soup from leftover beans, puree (pulverize) various foods for a better blend in recipes, and lots of other neat things. Be sure to keep the lid on when operating one or you may get a face full of tomato.

Food Processor

Be wary in the use of food processors. They can be vicious. They can be great for making salads, slicing tomatoes, too, if you are afraid of a sharp knife, chopping onions in a way to make you less teary-eyed, and getting other things ready for the cooking pot. Always follow the directions. These things can be meaner than a scared cat. If you get your fingers down in there you are a useless HouseHusband ever afterwards. And speaking of onions, if you don't watch out you can turn a perfectly honest onion into nearly unrecognizable juice.

Electric Knife

You used to think that this was just a tool to fillet fish, right? WRONG. Now you use it to slice roast really thin, the way an Uppity Woman likes it, or turkey, or chicken, or duck, or...whatever.

Electric knives are simple enough to use. Most models have a set of blades that measure about five inches and seven inches respectively. You might as well throw away the shorter one. You will gravitate to the longer blade instinctively because it gives you more leverage and control. Don't "saw" with an electric Knife, as you must with a conventional knife to cut anything; let the instrument "saw" for itself and you will receive a smoother cut.

Electric Skillet

This tool is useful in making pancakes, frying bacon or eggs, scrambling eggs (especially if you are doing about two dozen at a time for the Uppity Woman's brunch), or just about anything requiring controlled heat that will fit into the thing. It does get hot, so do not handle it directly while cooking.

Electric Popcorn Popper

Useful for making after-dinner snacks for the Uppity Woman. The preferred model is an air-popper mostly because it is easier (you just pour the corn down the shaft, put on the lid, place a bowl under the chute, and wait). Be sure to put the lid on or corn will go all over the kitchen. Ditto the bowl under the chute. You'd be surprised how fast those little suckers can decorate the floor if you are careless.

Electric Grill

You may never need this, but if you are preparing for the Uppity Woman's brunch (mentioned above) you can fry a lot of bacon at one time using this.

Electric Warming Grill

See Electric Grill. Good for keeping biscuits or other breads warm, too.

26

Microwave Oven

The publisher said I had to include this, and I suppose I should. Actually, I use mine only for two things: to defrost frozen meat and warm up last night's leftovers for lunch. For these two functions such devices are marvels. In five or six minutes they can defrost an item that would require several hours by the natural process. Warming foods is much less expensive and quicker in the microwave. If you want to actually *cook* foods in one, I suggest you do not begin with the "boiled egg" as did my friend Angela. Too many times microwaves turn an ordinary egg into a bomb. Then you must scrape the "shrapnel" from all sides of the cube.

Hand Operated Kitchen Tools

Knives

Every HouseHusband must have several varieties of knives, each with its special function. One uniform rule holds that all must be sharp to function properly. Remember: dull knives hurt more when you cut your finger.

A knife retains some residue of whatever you cut and as you move from food to food this may not be desirable. Residue makes little difference with vegetables, but try fish or onions. The odor will linger.

You will need several paring knives (short handled, short bladed) to open packages, pry up the edges of cans, and stab into a roast to see if it is done.

A tapered slicing knife is the handiest thing in the kitchen. It slices the fat off meat, makes thin slices of tomatoes or other vegetables, or anything else that can be cut. I even use it to "chop" onions into slices by drawing it across the cross-sections of the onion. It is a good idea to have a clean towel handy when your eyes start to tear.

You really are supposed to "chop" onions (peppers too) with a chopping knife, a broad bladed critter that looks a little like a Bowie knife. You firmly rock the thing back and forth and it evenly cuts whatever.

Then there is the butcher knife if you ever need to butcher anything. A word of caution here: knives should never be pointed at anything you don't intend to cut. It is best to keep

27

them out of the hands of Uppity Women, for several reasons. They are liable, for example, to cut their cultured nails.

Cutting Board

This goes with knives. You do not want to make little notches in your formica counter top every time you cook. This is most annoying to former cooks (*nee* Uppity Women) who retain a nostalgic and proprietary attitude toward the kitchen. If you are lucky, your son made a cutting board in woodworking; otherwise they are available in houseware departments.

Spoons

One thing you will notice is that there are never enough spoons.You will need an unlimited supply of them to stir things and, even worse than knives, they retain odor and food residue. Change them often. You will need at least one large slotted spoon to lift things from liquid, a large solid spoon when you want the liquid to be lifted, several plastic and/or wooden spoons to use with Teflon-coated pots and pans, and as many smaller serving spoons as possible. In a tight squeeze they double as shoe horns.

Spatula

You will need at least four: a Teflon spatula to lift eggs from a Teflon frying pan so you won't scratch the pan; a solid long-handled spatula to use on the grill; a short-handled spatula to turn cornbread in an iron skillet; and a rubber spatula to get as much of the ingredients as possible out of a bowl.

Tongs

You will need at least two because it is McDonald's Law Number One that one is always dirty. They are useful for removing frying things out of the grease and, if there is company for dinner, for putting ice in drinking glasses. Otherwise it is faster to use your hands.

Can Opener

Only sissies and Uppity Women use electric can openers. HouseHusbands use the crank variety. If the opener is heavy enough, it can double as a hammer should you need one in the kitchen.

Timer

Since nearly everything that cooks must be timed, at least at first. Experienced HouseHusbands develop a sixth sense about this. Yet, a timer with a bell can be a useful device. A wall clock or wristwatch can give the time, of course, providing you remember what time you started a thing and what time it is supposed to end. But they are silent. So a timer can give you a bell-like reminder when a given period of time is up, providing you remember to set it.

Ladles

At least two are required for the same reason cited for tongs. This is the only way to serve soup or skim off excess fluid, providing there is enough of it. Can you imagine doing this with a mere spoon, an activity that resembles scrubbing dirty pots with a toothbrush?

Potato Peeler

Every kitchen needs three: one is in the dishwasher, one is lost, and one works. Peelers are useful on carrots, cucumbers, or whatever needs peeling; but watch your thumbnail when peeling a skinny carrot. Left-handed models are available. Honest.

Egg Ring

This instrument becomes necessary only if your Uppity Woman likes neat eggs. You place the ring in the skillet and try your best to get the yolk and white to drop into the ring. The result is a completely symmetrical circle made of egg. The really skilled HouseHusband can even center the yolk.

Bacon Press

Same as above. Bacon tends to curl and then it does not cook evenly. Some Uppity Women won't eat curly bacon.

Measuring Cups and Spoons

You will need a one-cup, two-cup, and four-cup measurer, probably two of each if possible. They are handy for storing chopped or measured ingredients until the moment of truth.

Measuring spoons are equally vital. If they are not available, you can just make an educated guess on almost everything except chili powder. But remember: it is a lot easier to add salt, pepper, or tobasco, than to get it out.

Grater

No knife in the world can really grate properly, and a potato peeler, despite its marvelous quality of diversity, is too slow. Graters provide the only way to get grated cheese from a block of the stuff. Most stores now sell grated cheese in packages, so you may not need this.

Colander

You must have at least two, preferably three. See Tongs and Ladles. You can wash vegetables in them, steam vegetables in them if the pot is large enough, drain spaghetti in them and, in a bind, store cut vegetables in them. They might be used as a helmet in a moment of domestic crisis, too.

Pots and Pans

Stainless steel pots are best. They stay cleaner looking, do not pit, and are the most durable. You may never have to replace them if you start with high-quality pots and pans.

You will need a small one-quart pot, a larger two-quart pot, a still larger four-quart pot, and a giant pot. You are not likely to prepare more than four dishes at a time, so this should be sufficient unless you like to have a lot of them around to hang on the wall. Experienced HouseHusbands, and even fastidious Uppity Women, regard pot hangings as pure affectation. It is trying to look French, and what Real American wants to do that? Hanging pots on the kitchen wall is not as bad as hanging pantyhose on the shower door to dry, but it is getting close.

Have as many pots and pans as you wish, but not so many that you cannot hide them in cabinets.

You will need a Teflon-coated frying pan for frying bacon and eggs and sautéing. You may need a lid for it, but you can probably "borrow" one from your giant pot.

Casserole Dishes

Probably two 9 x 13 x 2 inch dishes and a smaller one will be adequate. Most HouseHusbands will not make that many casseroles at one time anyway. You might like a fancy round one for serving at the Uppity Woman's brunch.

Scissors

Every kitchen needs scissors to open packaged food and clip coupons and recipes from the newspaper. Try pasting the recipes in the back of this book.

Meat Mallet

Metal mallets with pointy edges are available to beat the tar out of round steak. The edge of a saucer will do, but it might break and cut your hand. Like the can opener, it can double as a hammer.

Apron

This symbolizes your circumstance. You do not need fancy hats, gloves (other than pot holders for handling hot dishes and pans), or even special shoes, although comfortable shoes are desirable when standing and waiting for the water to boil. You will need an apron. Get one of the grocery-clerk or butcher-shop kind, and if possible, have someone needlepoint "HouseHusband" on the bib. Fancy little things with flowers or butterflies on them are demeaning and nonfunctional anyway. Get a BIG one, especially because HouseHusbands are nearly always messy. This will protect your tie, white shirt, and suit pants as you cook.

This is far short from an exhaustive list. Indeed, it lists only the bare necessities of a functioning kitchen. If you have most of these things, you will be able to prepare all the recipes in this book.

Shopping

Before you can cook something, you have to get it to the kitchen. It is a good idea to keep a pad handy in the kitchen to jot down items of which you have just used the last portion. Take an inventory of the pantry. If this is your first time, it is likely that your Uppity Woman has not kept it stocked adequately since she has been too busy with other things. You will need all kinds of spices, packages, cans, and frozen things. Look at the recipes you want to cook and make sure these things are on your list if not in the pantry.

Take the checkbook to the supermarket with you. You are in for a shock, what with inflation and all. Tomatoes are likely to be somewhere just under a dollar a pound, and a pound of hamburger will cost about two bucks. After several trips you will have the floor plan pattern down pretty well, but do not be sheepish about asking stocking clerks the location of things.

Other shoppers can be helpful. Be careful about this. Someone told me that according to *Playboy Magazine* or some such publication, supermarkets bring more people together than do singles bars. Either *she* or *he* (it is a new world, remember) will think *you* want more than directions, or *they* may want to give *you* more than directions. Remember that most women are or will become Uppity, so if you want to save yourself a lot of difficulty, just say "thank you" and aim your shopping cart toward whatever it was you wanted.

Now it strikes me that I ought to say right about here that I have never experienced such a circumstance in either a supermarket or a bar. Honest. I guess those things only happen to the Beautiful People.

I might add that just about the time you have the floor plan of the grocery store memorized, they will hire a new whiz kid in marketing to turn the store upside down. Bread is now where beans belong, and toilet paper occupies the shelf that formerly displayed seasonings and spices. This is most annoying, and no amount of complaining to the manager will do any good because She takes Her orders from Headquarters.

Anyway, I find it useful to shop the produce section first because I prefer to use fresh vegetables and besides, this is the department that usually is located next to where you find the store personnel has stored the shopping carts. McDonald's Law

Number Two holds that the first cart in the line will be jammed so tightly into the second cart that not even Arnold Schwarzenegger could pry them apart. This will not be apparent when you innocently stroll up to the cart. It becomes revealed only by your struggle, which is invariably witnessed by three impatient unliberated women, four assistant managers who act as if you jammed the carts together, and a child of two who giggles. Be cool. Calmly offer the carts to the women and ignore the assistant managers and the child. Then get the *third* cart and proceed to the vegetables.

I place vegetables in the kiddie seat to keep the tomatoes or delicate fruit from being crushed. Then comes the canned goods, meats, dairy products, household cleaning items, and last, the bread. This deliberate and scientific approach is likely to be undone by the sacker who will be sure the bread and strawberries go under a gallon of milk and a five-pound sack of flour. I don't have a recipe for Strawberry Bread. This doesn't happen too often but you should look out for it anyway.

It is a good thing to have a clean handkerchief with you when you check out. When you see that the figure on the register tape totals $134.96, your palms will sweat and smudge the ink on the check. Take care of this kind of thing. Sweaty palms do not come in the same league with forgetting to use deodorant, but it *is* embarrassing.

It is possible to gauge the inflation rate by shopping for groceries. I remember when you could get about $5 worth of groceries in a sack. The sack is the same size but it easily handles $20 worth of groceries these days. Maybe the groceries have shrunk.

A Word About Fat

When I assumed the cooking duties at our place some years back, I cooked as I had learned, using bacon drippings (the grease rendered from frying bacon), ham, or even raw bacon itself, to make every vegetable taste better. Butter, or at least margarine, gave something special to a fried egg. And fried anything was quicker, and often tastier, than any other way of preparing food.

One thing an Uppity Woman will show quicker than her college degree or business card is her desire to keep a good thing going. She doesn't want to have to go back to cooking because her cook dies of a heart attack, or, in most cases, go to the trouble of finding a replacement. It takes too much time away from more important things. In our case, my Uppity Woman gave me a complete physical examination by an internist for my birthday present. At first I thought that was an unusual present, but I went along with the idea because I had not had a checkup in about a decade.

Now her choice of doctors turned out to be a fanatic. Oh, he smiled a lot during the examination to trick me. He strapped me down and attached wires all over my body while an assistant sucked blood out of my arm with a needle. He had me do all kinds of unpleasant things, and after an hour or so came to the conclusion that I had fifteen pounds more of me than was really necessary. FAT, he called it. Then the results of the blood sucking came back, and the report said that I had too much FAT in my blood.

So Dr. Joe gave me the bad news. I said he was a fanatic, so it should come as no surprise that the first thing he told me to do was lose the fifteen pounds. How? By exercise, which he translated into a brisk walk of two to three miles a day at a clip of about one mile every fifteen minutes. When I really got into exercise, he said, I ought to drop the time to about thirteen minutes per mile. He told me to stop eating so much FAT and some of the FAT would leave my blood and the rest of my body.

The point of revealing all this personal and somewhat embarrassing information (fifteen pounds of FAT, indeed!), is that I was in the middle of this cookbook when this bad news came. I had my recipes loaded with bacon, ham, butter, cream, cheese, whole milk, and many other things that I thought made things taste good. What I learned is that I was mostly tasting FAT, not food.

Now I am not a reformer, so what I have decided to do since the publisher made me revise this sociological statement anyway, is to have my cake and eat it too, with apologies to Dr. Joe, who has forbidden me to eat cake. Where possible, I have given you the OLD WAY *and* the NEW WAY to cook. The OLD WAY saw many of my relatives through eighty or ninety summers, so it wasn't too bad for them. But then they worked on farms and in factories and did other active things and besides, they didn't know any better, so it didn't hurt them. Since I know better, the FAT would kill me. So much for dangerous information.

A funny thing happened as a result of the Great Reform. I stopped putting so much FAT in my mouth and in my gut-on-the-inside, and about twenty pounds of FAT came off the outside. Now we are not through with problems. When you lose twenty pounds, people think you are sick and ask what is wrong with you. If you say Dr. Joe made me do it, then they understand that the whole thing was not your idea and they forgive you, although a few friends will still delight in eating nachos and pizza right in your face. They are sadists who enjoy blowing smoke in the face of someone trying to quit smoking. That kind of person likes cats and speaks French.

Another problem arises when your clothes don't fit anymore. You take to suspenders until you can get to the alterations person at the cleaners or department store. Your clothes will never fit correctly again, of course, and your rear pants pockets now spread about an inch and a half apart.

Ignore these minor irritations. Great is your reward. Your Uppity Woman starts to wonder if, in your svelte condition, you might be attractive to other Uppity Women and may start paying more attention to you. Or maybe not, but *you* know you look better, and that counts for a lot.

The point here: if you want to use the bacon drippings and cheese and stuff, and you are a consenting adult, you will find such things listed in the recipes. If you don't want to use them, you will find alternative ways of cooking that will be just as tasty. And then once a month you can go to the pizza parlor and pig out.

1

Meats,
Main Dishes,
and
Casseroles

Vegeterianism is fine, if you want to limit yourself to plants, but most HouseHusbands still want meat on the table. It isn't necessary to have meat every meal or even every day, but you need not let your innards forget that there is something besides potatoes and green beans in the world to eat.

Once upon a time at our house that would have meant bacon with breakfast, at least two slices of lunch meat (bologna or ham, probably) in a sandwich at noon, and steak or roast for dinner. Dr. Joe ended all that for me. Now I have learned the lower-fat advantage of poultry and fish, especially the cold water variety of fish, and never, never to fry any of it. Now I mostly bake meat with barbecue sauce, being careful to read the labels so the sauce doesn't have "hydrogenated" anything in it. Such is the nature of middle age.

Our boys still like red meat, my Uppity Woman's cholesterol ranks so low she could eat raw bacon laced with gooey cheese and not have to worry, and probably most of you still enjoy your steak, roast, bacon, or ham (with cheese). For the sake of providing a little something for all HouseHusbands, you will find quite a few high-fat, high-cholesterol recipes in the following pages on meat, but occasionally I will slip in a low-fat, low-cholesterol alternative.

Either way you like it — low or high — you have assumed the responsibility for having dinner on the table when the Uppity Woman gets home. Old-fashioned as most of us are, that will mean some kind of meat dish. Consider the following possibilities. The menu section provides recommendations on how to alternate the recipes, and what to serve with them.

For now, let's just ease into this thing. Don't put on your apron yet. You don't even have to go to the kitchen to read the recipes to select what you wish to prepare. If you are an old hand who is just looking for a few new recipes, or if you are a Kitchen Virgin, as it were, you should look at this book in the most comfortable place. That will be the recliner chair, which faces the fireplace and the television set, with a convenient reading lamp beside it. You know, the chair where formerly you waited for your Little Woman to prepare the meal. If your new Uppity Woman has commandeered the area for business use, you may have to go into the garage to find a quiet place.

Wherever you read the book, by all means do read it. It can save you time. After all, where else could you find a cookbook that gives recommendations on making you fatter and thinner in the same recipe?

A.P.'s Sirloin Special

Did you notice the cute use of the initials on this one? Actually I am claiming undue credit: my Uppity Woman taught me this one early in the game, or back in the old days when I consumed all the red meat I wanted. For those of you who still can, this one is a good beginner. For the rest, well, chew a carrot stick and keep reading.

Ingredients:

12-16 ounce sirloin steak
1-2 packages Lipton Onion Mushroom Soup,
**   depending upon number to be served**
Worcestershire Sauce
Garlic Salt

Preparation:

1. About six hours before cooking, sprinkle Onion Mushroom Soup mix over steak.
2. Sprinkle with garlic salt.
3. Sprinkle with enough Worcestershire sauce to make a liquidy paste of the soup on the steak.
4. Let soak in refrigerator until ready to cook.
5. Cook over charcoal briquettes or on outside gas grill.
6. For "medium well steak," cook about 10 minutes per side.
7. When you turn the meat, pour additional liquid of soup mix from marinating over top to keep moist.

Goes very well with baked potato and a simple garden salad.

Baked Hash

You can prepare this quickly. This recipe has a masculine aspect, but remember your Uppity Woman will eat everything you cook for fear that you will quit cooking if she doesn't.

Ingredients:

4 cups chopped roast or other meat
1 onion, chopped
1/2 teaspoon Worcestershire sauce
1 1/2 tablespoons butter or margarine
1/2 teaspoon salt
1/4 teaspoon pepper
1/2 teaspoon Kitchen Bouquet
1/4 cup flour
2 carrots, cut into 1-inch pieces
1 cup water

Preparation:

1. Place all ingredients in baking dish.
2. Bake at 350 degrees for about 1 hour.

Beef Stew

Stew is especially good on a cold day, and you can make an abundance so you can heat it up a bowl at a time in your Microwave, if you have one. This is especially useful on days when the Uppity Woman has a business lunch and you are left to eat alone.

Ingredients:

1 pound stew meat
4 to 6 potatoes, cut in chunks
4 to 6 carrots, peeled and cut in chunks
1 can cut green beans
1 small can tomatoes
1/2 bell pepper, cut in strips
1/2 onion, cut in chunks
1/4 to 1/2 cup cooking oil
Salt to taste
Black pepper to taste
**Optional: Just about any leftover vegetable in the
    refrigerator.**

Preparation:

1. Peel and cut potatoes, carrots, onion, and pepper.
2. Salt and pepper meat.
3. Flour stew meat on all sides.
4. Pour oil in large pot, heat.
5. Brown meat on all sides, remove meat and drain oil from pot.
6. Reduce heat to Low-to-Medium.
7. Return meat to pot, add water to cover about 3/4 inch.

8. Add: potatoes, carrots, tomatoes, onions, salt, and pepper.
9. Cover and cook 45 minutes, stirring occasionally.
10. Add green beans.
11. A few minutes later add strips of bell pepper.
12. Add water if necessary to keep from becoming too dry.
13. Taste in about ten minutes and serve when the potatoes and carrots are easily pierced by a fork.

Accompanies: Stove Top Corn Bread

Brunswick Stew, Texas Style

This is a fine old Virginia recipe, from Pat Butler, which should be made in quantity and can be frozen. Originally, the recipe called for squirrel or rabbit in addition to the chicken. If you have access to this meat, use it along with the chicken in a ratio of two parts chicken to one part game.

Ingredients:

2 pounds of chicken parts
Water
1 meaty ham bone or 1/4 pound bacon
2 large cans Rotel tomatoes
2 packages frozen lima beans
2 packages frozen white corn
1 pound potatoes, diced
1 stalk celery, chopped
2 yellow onions, chopped
1 package frozen okra
3/4 clove of garlic
2 tablespoons marjoram
3 to 5 dashes of Tabasco sauce
4 to 6 tablespoons of Worcestershire sauce
4 tablespoons brown sugar
4 ounces good bourbon
4 tablespoons flour

Preparation:

1. In a large pot, add the chicken or chicken/game mixture. Cover with water, bring to a boil and simmer for about 40 minutes.
2. Remove chicken from the pot, bone, and return the meat to the pot.

3. Add: ham bone or bacon (if ham bone is used, remove meat from the bone into the stew and remove bone after 2 hours of simmering; if bacon is used, chop it and add to the stew as it simmers), Rotel tomatoes, lima beans, white corn, potatoes, celery, onions, okra, garlic, marjoram, Tabasco sauce, Worcestershire sauce, brown sugar, bourbon.
4. Simmer gently for about 3 hours.
5. About 30 minutes before the end of cooking time, remove a cup of the liquid and mix with the flour.
6. Pour this mixture back into the stew and stir.
7. This will thicken it slightly.

This is a soupy stew and is wonderful the second day. It freezes well. Serve it with a salad and some bread.

Celestial Spaghetti

*Now this one I learned watching television one Saturday after-
noon. The David Wade Show. See what kind of TV will interest
you now? For me, it used to be ball games, now it's the David
Wade Show. Never, never watch Donahue or Winfrey unless you
are in the hospital.*

*I made a few changes in the recipe to suit my taste, but I do
believe ol' David would make the world's best HouseHusband, as
far as cooking is concerned. He looks so good while he is working.
After making this delicacy, my kitchen looks as if the Three
Stooges and crew have just finished filming a scene there. Pots
are all dirty, there is a mess everywhere, and even the floor needs
mopping. But it is worth it. This is the best spaghetti you will ever
eat, even if you did cook it yourself.*

Ingredients:

1 package spaghetti (20 ounce)
2 pounds ground beef (or turkey)
1 to 2 onions, chopped
1 bell pepper, chopped
1 6-ounce can mushrooms
1 6-ounce can tomato paste
1 can tomato sauce
1 can tomatoes, mashed
1 teaspoon salt
1/2 teaspoon dry mustard
1/2 teaspoon oregano
1/2 teaspoon black pepper
1/4 teaspoon garlic powder
1/4 teaspoon Tabasco sauce
1/2 teaspoon chili powder
1/4 teaspoon Worcestershire (powder or sauce)

Preparation:

1. Cook spaghetti for 15 minutes in boiling water. Drain.
2. As spaghetti cooks, start to brown ground meat in large pot.
3. As meat browns, add— stirring in— each of the remaining ingredients.
4. Stir in spaghetti. Sauce should be ample to dominate spaghetti.
5. May be eaten at this point. However, for finer blending, bake at 375 degrees for 30 to 40 minutes.

Should Serve a Party!

Chicken Fried Steak

This is the old Southern, especially Texas, stand-by. Please don't spoil it by using catsup or Worchestershire sauce on it. Learn to make a gravy at least. I don't make the fancy cream gravy found in restaurants. Try my gravy recipe.

Ingredients:

2 pounds round steak
3 tablespoons sugar
1/2 teaspoon Creole seasoning
1 egg
1 tablespoon baking powder
2 cups milk
1 to 2 cups cooking oil
Flour

Preparation:

1. Cut all fat from meat.
2. Tenderize meat by pounding with a mallet or edge of saucer.
3. Cut into pieces about 5 to 6 inches in width.
4. In a bowl combine: sugar, Creole seasoning, egg, baking powder, milk.
5. Mix until ingredients are smooth.
6. Flour all sides of meat.
7. Dip in batter until all sides are wet.
8. Remove and flour all sides again.
9. Heat oil.
10. Fry until brown, about 8 minutes.

Chicken Fried Steak Gravy

Ingredients:

3 tablespoons cooking oil
3 tablespoons flour
2 cups water
Salt
Pepper

Preparation:

1. Pour vegetable oil to cover the bottom of an iron skillet.
2. Heat until quite hot, but not "popping."
3. While oil heats, get about 2 cups of tap water in a measuring cup and keep it handy.
4. When oil is hot, reduce heat to medium, sift flour into skillet.
5. Stir flour, oil, and salt constantly until mixture is quite brown.
6. Add water gradually, stirring constantly until you get thickness you like, and allow gravy to boil. (Avoid steamed glasses by using a long-armed approach.)
7. Stir to insure smooth blending. Add salt and pepper to taste. When this is done, you may pour it over the steak when served. There is no hope for cholesterol-watchers on this one so, if you eat it, enjoy. You can feel patriotic tonight and repent tomorrow.

Corn "Willie"

This is another "gift" from an anonymous soul who must have helped out when I didn't want to start over on Emmie's recipes the very next day.

Ingredients:

1 pound ground beef (or turkey)
1 onion, chopped
1 large can whole kernel corn, drained
1 large can tomatoes
Salt and pepper

Preparation:

1. Brown ground meat until almost done (it will be still pink). Pour off excess grease.
2. Add: onions, tomatoes, corn, salt and pepper.
3. Mix together.
4. Simmer for 15 minutes, or until meat is done.

Emmie's Ground Beef Casserole #1

Emmie Peacock is a gorgeous lady who used to work down the hall from my office. Emmie tried to pretend that she longed for the domestic life, and used such excuses for working as the need to pay the tuition of her three daughters and one son to go to college. Since some of them went to Texas A&M, and Emmie is a devout Republican, I knew all along that she had plenty of money; she just wanted to get out in the work place so she could tell Bill she was independent. Anyway, Emmie was my salvation in the days when I was a Freshman HouseHusband. On days when ideas for dinner did not came easily, about 4 p.m. I would walk down the hall to Emmie's office and ask for help. That girl knows more ways to prepare ground beef (or turkey, remember) than the American Beef Institute. The next three recipes are a tribute to her ingenuity – and her desire to get dinner over with quickly so she can play bridge. They are tasty, especially #3, if you like the Mexican flavors.

Ingredients:

1 pound ground beef (or turkey)
1 can Veg-All
1 8-ounce can tomato sauce
1 can tomato puree

Preparation:

1. Brown ground meat.
2. Pour off grease.
3. Add and stir in: Veg-All, tomato sauce, tomato puree.
4. Add water if necessary to keep mixture from being dry.
5. Cover and cook 15 minutes at Low-Medium heat.

Emmie's Ground Beef Casserole #2

Ingredients:

1 pound ground beef (or turkey)
2 to 3 cans (small) tomato sauce
2 cups uncooked rice
1 1/2 cups water
1 teaspoon salt
1/4 teaspoon pepper

Preparation:

1. Brown ground meat.
2. Pour off grease.
3. Add and stir in: tomato sauce, rice, salt, pepper.
4. Reduce heat to Medium-Low, cover, cook 15 to 20 minutes or until rice is done.

Emmie's Ground Beef Casserole #3

Ingredients:

1 pound ground beef (or turkey)
1 can chili beans
1 can enchilada sauce
1 cup grated cheese

Preparation:

1. Brown ground meat.
2. Pour off grease.
3. Add and stir in: chili beans, enchilada sauce.
4. Cover and cook 5 to 10 minutes at medium heat.
5. Add cheese.
6. Cook until cheese melts.

Enchilada Squares

You can tell by now that I am partial to Mexican food, or at least that cuisine known as Tex-Mex. This one is easy and can feed unexpected company that your Uppity Woman brings home. Just add enough corn chips and it will stretch a long way.

Ingredients:

1 pound ground beef (or turkey)
4 eggs, beaten
1 8-ounce can tomato sauce
1/4 cup chopped onion
1 small can evaporated milk
1 can enchilada sauce
1 cup grated cheese
2 cups Frito corn chips

Preparation:

1. Mix in a bowl: beaten eggs, milk, tomato sauce, enchilada sauce.
2. Brown ground meat.
3. Pour off grease.
4. Sauté onions in skillet with meat.
5. Put sautéed meat and onions into a 9 x 12 x 2-inch baking dish.
6. Pour egg/milk mixture over meat and mix.
7. Top with corn chips.
8. Bake uncovered at 350 degrees for 25 minutes.
9. Remove and sprinkle cheese over top.
10. Return to oven for 3 to 5 minutes or until cheese is bubbly.

Eye of Round Roast

This is the favorite Sunday "dinner," as we say in the South, at our place. This means we eat it about one p.m., after Sunday morning church. I should admit that this is the one meal each week that my Uppity Woman condescends to cook. This is mostly to keep up appearances since our two boys, who now live away from home, return each Sunday to perpetuate the ritual that Mother Cooks. When she is too busy, she lets me do this one, too, because it is truly difficult to mess up.

Ingredients:

Eye of round roast, 3 to 4 pounds
Seasoned pepper
Seasoned salt
Garlic powder
Worcestershire sauce

Preparation:

1. Defrost roast if necessary.
2. Sprinkle generously with: seasoned pepper, seasoned salt, garlic powder, Worcestershire sauce.
3. Bake at 275 degrees for 1 hour and 20 minutes.

Freida's Pepper Beef

This dandy came from Mrs. Freida Johnson, who is the wife of my main boss. I am privileged to work in an industry that provides me with four direct-line bosses, each with absolute veto power over everything I do, and I work for them in an era when the United States Supreme Court has endorsed the principle that it is appropriate to hire women over men even if they have less experience and score lower on qualifying tests, because in the end we will have a better society. Or something like that. These bosses — all males who got their jobs before the Supreme Court spoke— are nice enough, but best of all they have nice spouses who await the arrival of this book. My only concern is that if they give copies and demand that their spouses become HouseHusbands too, that I may get vetoed a lot more often.

Ingredients:

1 brisket of beef, 4 to 5 pounds
1/2 cup black pepper, coarsely ground (cut down
     on this next time if it proves too much for
     you)
Marinade:
2 cups soy sauce
1 1/2 cups vinegar
3 tablespoons catsup
3 teaspoons paprika
3 cloves garlic, pressed

Preparation:

1. To make marinade, combine: soy sauce, vinegar, catsup, paprika, pressed garlic. Mix well.
2. Marinate brisket for two nights, or at least 48 hours before cooking.

3. When ready to prepare, place a large piece of wax paper on cabinet or table.
4. Spread black pepper evenly on wax paper.
5. Lift brisket from marinade and shake off excess liquid, but do not dry.
6. Place brisket on pepper on wax paper.
7. Pat top side so pepper will stick to bottom.
8. Turn meat over and pat again so other side will absorb pepper.
9. Wrap in foil.
10. Bake at 300 degrees for 3 hours.
11. Slice thin and serve.

Freida says this is good served cold the next day.

Goulash

I can't recall where this one came from. As Yogi Berra says, "If you like this sort of thing, this is definitely the sort of thing you will like."

Ingredients:

1 pound ground beef (or turkey)
1 bell pepper, chopped
1 onion, chopped
1 can chili beef soup (or chili powder to taste and
     2 cups water)
1 can whole kernel corn
1 8-ounce package of macaroni

Preparation:

1. Cook macaroni in boiling water, according to directions on package, about 15 minutes or until tender.
2. Brown ground meat.
3. Pour off grease.
4. Add: peppers, onions, chili soup (or chili powder and water).
5. Stir and cook until hot.
6. Add: corn, drained; cooked macaroni, drained.
7. Stir thoroughly and serve.

Gypsy Rice B.

This came from one of my counterparts, HH Greg Beil. Greg is a sometime probation officer, full-time HouseHusband, and restorer of old houses to boot. His Uppity Woman, Gail, is involved in everything in their town.

Ingredients:

1 onion, chopped
1/2 stick butter or margarine
1 pound ground beef (or turkey)
2 beef bouillon cubes
2 cups water, hot
1 1/4 cup rice
1 tablespoon Worcestershire sauce, or to taste
1 tablespoon soy sauce, or to taste

Preparation:

1. Melt butter in pan.
2. Add onions and sauté.
3. Add ground meat and brown.
4. Dissolve beef bouillon cubes in water and add to meat mixture.
5. Stir in rice.
6. Add: Worcestershire sauce, soy sauce.
7. Cover and simmer for 30 minutes, or until rice is done.

Italian Swiss Steak

I forgot where I got this one, but you don't have to be Italian or Swiss to enjoy it.

Ingredients:

1/4 cup flour
1 teaspoon salt (add more if you like salt)
1/4 teaspoon pepper
3 tablespoons vegetable oil, preferably safflower
     oil
2 pounds round steak
1 8-ounce can seasoned tomato sauce
1 5 1/2-ounce or smaller can of pizza sauce
1/2 cup water
1/2 teaspoon sugar
1/2 teaspoon oregano
1 onion sliced or chopped

Preparation:

1. Combine flour, salt, pepper.
2. Pound into steak.
3. Pour oil into iron skillet.
4. Brown meat on both sides.
5. Add over meat: tomato sauce, pizza sauce, water, sugar, oregano.
6. Top with onion.
7. Cover and bake at 350 degrees for 1 hour or until tender.

Leftover Oriental Disguise

This is another of Greg Beil's contributions.

Ingredients:

1 tablespoon cooking oil
2 cups cooked rice
2 small onions, chopped
1 tomato (preferably fresh), peeled and cut up
2 cups meat (chicken, beef, or pork), chopped
1 egg
1 tablespoon soy sauce, or to taste

Preparation:

1. Heat oil in a skillet.
2. Sauté onions and meat until onions are clear.
3. Add: tomato, rice, soy sauce.
4. Simmer until hot.
5. Push ingredients in skillet to the back.
6. Fry egg for a few seconds.
7. Before the egg gets hard, mix it with rest of ingredients.
8. Cook another minute or so.

Linda's Chili

Linda is another former student of mine. Her husband, Jerry Cross, is in the construction business and raises cattle. Linda is a typical old-fashioned girl, and even claims that Jerry is unliberated. All she does is teach a full load plus overload classes at a college, serve as president of about five organizations, does church work, has written a book, and is learning to waltz. Now I ask you, is that old fashioned or is that old fashioned? I don't know about Jerry.

Ingredients:

**2 pounds ground beef or turkey (deer meat is
       good, claims Linda)**
1/2 onion, diced
1 pound red beans, cooked
2 pints tomato juice
2 small cans tomato sauce
1 can stewed tomatoes
1 jar Heinz chili sauce
1 teaspoon chili powder
1/4 teaspoon cumin
1/4 teaspoon cayenne pepper
Salt and pepper to taste
Water as desired

Preparation:

1. Cook red beans. Prepare according to directions on package in advance.
2. In pan, sauté onion and meat.
3. Drain off fat.
4. Mix into meat mixture:
   red beans, tomato juice, tomato sauce, stewed tomatoes, chili sauce, chili powder, cumin, cayenne pepper, salt and pepper.
5. Simmer for 30 to 45 minutes.

Mean Chili

"Mean" is right. Cut back a little on the seasoning if you have a delicate stomach. (Delicate means that even a little chili seasonings burn your mouth. If it burns there, you can bet it will later in the belly. Of course, "fire in the belly" has a different meaning and we are not discussing politics in this book, at least not directly.) If you don't have a delicate stomach, and you are like my friend Tom Choate, whose very name is a French word that means "hot" throw in a little Tabasco sauce. I told you not to trust the French.

Ingredients:

4 pounds lean ground beef (or turkey)
2 pounds pork sausage (or turkey sausage)
4 onions, chopped (2 white, 2 yellow)
1 clove garlic, chopped
1/4 to 1/2 teaspoon chili powder
2 bell peppers, chopped
1 15 1/2-ounce jar of mushroom spaghetti sauce
1/2 teaspoon black pepper
1/2 cup chopped olives
1 3-ounce can tomato sauce
3 tablespoons butter or margarine

Preparation:

1. Brown ground meat and sausage together.
2. Drain off grease.
3. In separate pan, sauté in butter or margarine: onions, garlic, bell pepper.
4. Add the ground meat and stir in: spaghetti sauce, mushrooms, olives, tomato sauce.
5. Mix thoroughly.
6. Add chili powder to taste.

7. Add black pepper to taste.
8. You may add additional tomato sauce to obtain desired consistency.
9. You may want to add chopped jalapeño peppers or grated cheddar cheese. If so, add only a few pieces of jalapeño at a time to keep this thing from getting out of hand.

Old-Fashioned Meat Loaf

This one was one of the first dishes my Uppity Woman taught me to prepare. Caution! Do not take out of the oven too soon. You might like rare steak, but gooey ground anything is something else again.

Ingredients:

**1 to 2 pounds of ground beef, or ground turkey —
     you really can't taste the difference**
**2 eggs, beaten (Mix "yellow" and "white" vigor-
     ously in a small bowl with a fork if you don't
     care how much animal fat you consume. Use
     only the "white" if you have to watch this in
     your diet.)**
1/2 cup cracker crumbs
1 6-ounce can tomato paste
1/4 cup chopped onion
1/4 cup chopped bell pepper
1 teaspoon salt
1 small can tomato sauce

Preparation:

1. Mix in a large bowl: eggs, cracker crumbs, tomato paste, onion, bell pepper, salt and pepper.
2. Be sure to get an even mix.
3. Add ground beef (or turkey). Mix thoroughly.
4. Shape into a loaf in a narrow pan about 12 x
   7 1/2 x 2 inches.
5. Add tomato sauce to top.
6. Bake at 350 degrees for 1 hour and 15 minutes.

Meat Loaf

This recipe is a close cousin to the preceding recipe. It is a little quicker, which is helpful on days when the Uppity Woman has a meeting to attend and not much time to eat.

Ingredients:

1 1/2 pounds ground beef or turkey
2 eggs, beaten, use only white of egg if you wish
    to reduce fat
3/4 cup coarsely crushed saltines
1 cup milk (skim, if you don't want the butterfat)
1/2 cup Parmesan cheese, grated
1/4 cup onion, chopped
1 teaspoon Worcestershire sauce
1/2 teaspoon garlic salt
1/4 teaspoon basil leaves, crushed
3 tablespoons catsup

Preparation:

1. Combine together in a large mixing bowl: eggs, crushed saltines, milk, Parmesan cheese, onion, Worcestershire sauce, garlic salt, basil leaves.
2. Add ground beef.
3. Mix well.
4. Shape into 6 individual loaves.
5. Place in shallow baking dish.
6. Spread tops of loaves with catsup, some Parmesan cheese, and crushed basil leaves.
7. Bake at 350 degrees for 45 minutes.

Mexican Casserole

This recipe came from a student who prepared it as a class project. While others made maps from plywood and paste, this lady turned on her oven and turned out an excellent dish. When I learned to substitute ingredients to achieve a lower-fat result, I dropped the cheese and the cream of chicken soup (all that "hydrogenated" stuff, you know), and discovered that what I really like about the taste of most Mexican food is the corn tortilla. That you still have with this recipe.

Ingredients:

12 corn tortillas
2 pounds ground beef (or turkey)
3/4 teaspoon chili powder
1/8 teaspoon garlic powder
1 onion, chopped
2 cans pinto beans or chili beans
16 Velveeta cheese slices (optional)
1 can Rotel tomatoes
**1 can Cream of Chicken Soup or 1 cup picante
     sauce**

Preparation:

1. Line bottom of greased 9 x 13 x 2 inch dish with 6 tortillas.
2. Brown ground meat.
3. Pour off grease.
4. Season meat with chili powder, garlic powder, and salt.
5. Spread in layers on tortillas: ground meat, onions, beans, cheese slices.
6. Repeat layers.

7. Place six tortillas on top.
8. Mix soup with Rotel tomatoes and pour over top layer of tortillas. If you use the picante sauce, omit Rotel tomatoes and even chicken soup. You can stand just so much pepper!
9. Cover with foil and bake 1 hour and 10 minutes at 350 degrees.
10. Uncover last 15 minutes of baking time. Serve with Mexican salad, page 160. Mexican Corn Bread, page 171.

Mexican Corn Bread Casserole

This is another of Emmie's creations. Anything fast, man, Emmie is for it. She claims that she makes this a lot when Bill is out of town. I don't know what she makes when Bill is in town, and Bill hasn't yet admitted that he is a HouseHusband, so I don't know if he cooks.

Ingredients:

1 to 2 pounds ground beef (or turkey)
1 can pinto beans
1 can enchilada sauce
1 package corn bread mix (follow instructions on
     package), or Stove Top Corn Bread recipe

Preparation:

1. Brown ground meat in an iron skillet.
2. Pour off as much grease as possible.
3. Spread in 9 x 13 x 2 inch baking dish.
4. Add beans.
5. Add enchilada sauce.
6. Mix and spread evenly.
7. Add mixed corn bread batter.
8. Spread as evenly as possible on top.
9. Bake at 325 degrees about 30 minutes, or until corn bread is done.

Pepper Steak

This one really appealed to me in my steak-eating days. It came to me from my mother, who would have been Uppity if given the chance. Today I substitute turkey breast for the steak. What I really like, anyway, is all the additional ingredients, especially the tomatoes and peppers. Enough seasoning will make almost anything edible.

Ingredients:

3 pounds boneless chuck roast, cut into cubes
1 teaspoon seasoned salt
1 can tomatoes
2 bell peppers, chopped
1 onion, chopped
2 beef (or chicken if you substitute turkey)
      bouillon cubes
1 tablespoon Worcestershire sauce

Preparation:

1. Season meat with salt.
2. Place in bottom of a Crock-Pot.
3. Add: Tomatoes, bell pepper, onion, bouillon cubes, Worcestershire sauce.
4. Stir gently.
5. Slow cook on low for 6 to 8 hours.

May be served over rice, if desired.

Pepper Steak

Here is a more complicated version of the Pepper Steak. This is at the intermediate level of HouseHusbandry because you have to remember to get the rice ready.

Ingredients:

1 1/2 pounds round steak cut into strips
1 tablespoon paprika
2 cloves garlic
2 tablespoons margarine
1 cup onion slices
2 large tomatoes cut in 8 pieces
2 bell peppers cut in strips
1 cup beef broth
1/4 cup water
2 tablespoons corn starch
2 tablespoons soy sauce
3 cups hot cooked rice

Preparation:

1. Cook rice. See page 130.
2. Cut steak into strips.
3. Sprinkle steak with paprika and let it sit a while.
4. Brown steak in margarine with the garlic.
5. Add: onions, peppers.
6. Cook until vegetables are wilted.
7. Add: tomatoes, beef broth.
8. Cover and simmer for 15 minutes.
9. Blend: water, corn starch, soy sauce.
10. Pour over steak and stir.
11. Cook until gravy thickens and meat is done.
12. Serve over the rice.

Porcupines

At least this one changes the appearance of the omnipresent HouseHusband's standby — ground beef (turkey — you really can't taste the difference when you get all the seasoning in).

Ingredients:

1 pound of ground beef (or turkey)
1/2 cup uncooked rice
1 No. 2 can tomato juice
1 small onion, chopped
1 teaspoon salt
1 bell pepper, chopped
1/2 teaspoon pepper
1/4 teaspoon nutmeg

Preparation:

1. Mix all ingredients together thoroughly.
2. Roll into balls.
3. Place in baking dish and bake at 350 degrees until done.

Sour Cream Enchilada Casserole

This recipe came from Sylvia Hunt, a former student. If you analyze this commentary too closely, it may imply I have something cooking with a lot of "former students." Well, let's do the lady a favor and interpret that statement literally. Sylvia is an excellent cook.

Ingredients:

1 cup water
2 tablespoons picante sauce
12 corn tortillas
2 pounds ground beef (or turkey)
1 onion, chopped
1 to 1 1/2 teaspoon salt
1/8 teaspoon pepper
2 teaspoons ground cumin
1 tablespoon chili powder (or less if you don't like
    things too spicy)
1 teaspoon garlic powder
3/4 cup ripe olives, sliced
1/4 cup picante sauce
1/2 cup margarine
2 tablespoons all purpose flour
1 1/2 cups milk
1 16-ounce carton sour cream
1/2 pound cheddar cheese, shredded

Preparation:

1. Combine water and 2 tablespoons of picante sauce in a large shallow dish.
2. Place tortillas in picante sauce mixture.
3. Let stand 5 minutes.

4. Drain.
5. Cook ground meat and onions in a heavy skillet.
6. Drain off excess fat.
7. Stir in: salt, pepper, cumin, chili powder, garlic powder, olives, and the remainder of the picante sauce.
8. Simmer for 5 minutes.
9. Melt margarine in a heavy saucepan over low heat.
10. Add flour.
11. Stir until smooth.
12. Cook for 1 minute, stirring constantly.
13. Gradually add milk, cooking over medium heat until thick and bubbly.
14. Remove from heat.
15. Add sour cream.
16. Stir until well blended.
17. Place half of tortillas in a 9 x 13 x 2 baking dish.
18. Pour half of sour cream mixture over tortillas.
19. Spoon half of meat mixture evenly over sauce.
20. Sprinkle with half of the cheese.
21. Repeat layering with remaining ingredients, ending with cheese on top.
22. Bake at 375 degrees for 25 minutes.

Steak and Potato Casserole

I honestly don't remember where I got this one, so it probably came from one of the would-be Uppity Women at work. They are always helpful, and most are anxious to give a copy of this book to their husbands.

Ingredients:

2 pounds round steak
1/4 cup flour
2 tablespoons flour
1 teaspoon salt (or less if you don't like too much)
1/4 teaspoon pepper
2 tablespoons salad oil
3 medium carrots, peeled and sliced
8 medium potatoes, peeled and sliced
1 package onion soup mix
Parsley

Preparation:

1. Peel and slice carrots.
2. Peel and slice potatoes.
3. Trim fat from meat.
4. Cut meat into 8 pieces.
5. Mix: salt, pepper, 1/4 cup flour.
6. Work into meat.
7. Place meat in large skillet with oil.
8. Brown meat on both sides.
9. Arrange meat in 2-quart casserole dish.
10. Place carrots and potatoes on top.
11. Sprinkle the onion soup mix over dish.
12. Add enough water to keep the meat from sticking.

13. Cover and bake at 350 degrees for 45 minutes to one hour, or until potatoes, carrots, and meat are tender.
14. Remove and skim off fat.
15. Thicken gravy with 2 tablespoons flour mixed with 1/4 cup water.
16. Return to oven for 5 to 10 minutes.
17. Sprinkle parsley on top when served.

Steaks Patrick

This tends to be improvisational, says my good friend Pat Butler, and when done correctly is a wonderful way to prepare steak. In general, unless one can broil steaks outside over charcoal or mesquite where a very hot fire seals juices in the meat, the most flavorful steaks are those pan-fried at a high temperature. The juices that escape return to the meat or can be incorporated in a sauce that complements the steak in the best possible way. For the dispossessed, keep chewing carrots and keep reading.

Ingredients:

One steak per person, ranging from a 6 to 8-ounce filet to a 10 to 12-ounce (or more) ribeye or strip steak, depending on your appetite.
2 ounces peanut (or safflower) oil
Salt and pepper
1 tablespoon butter or margarine per steak
1 green onion per steak, chopped
2 tablespoons beef stock per steak
1/2 cup dry white wine
4 medium mushrooms per steak, sliced
Dash of Worcestershire sauce
Dash of Tabasco sauce
2 ounces Cognac per steak

Preparation:

1. Heat 1 to 2 ounces of peanut oil in a good heavy frying pan large enough to hold all the steaks placed in a single layer, plus room for some mushrooms.
2. Salt and pepper steaks to taste.
3. Place steaks in hot frying pan, searing quickly on

each side and then cook them for about 4 to 6 minutes more on each side.

4. Remove to a warm plate or a warming oven.
5. Drain off the fat from frying pan, leaving brown specks.
6. Add: butter and green onion and sauté until wilted.
7. Add: beef stock, wine.
8. Stir until pan juices combine with liquid.
9. Add: mushrooms, Worcestershire sauce, Tabasco sauce.
10. Cook briefly.
11. Move mushrooms to edge of pan and return steaks.
12. Heat quickly at high temperature.
13. Add Cognac.
14. Ignite Cognac with match, immediately. (This must be done quickly or the mushrooms will absorb the Cognac.)
15. When the flames die down, remove from heat and serve.

This is good with either a baked potato or wild rice.

Son of a Gun Stew

I got this one out of a book, but honestly, I can't remember which one. I would give credit if I could. I didn't want to leave it out because of the name, if nothing else. We have to assert ourselves sometimes.

Ingredients:

1 to 2 pounds ground beef (or turkey)
1 can green chilis or 1 can Rotel tomatoes
1 onion, chopped
1 can corn
1 can tomatoes
1/2 teaspoon oregano
1 teaspoon salt
1/2 teaspoon pepper

Preparation:

1. Brown ground meat in a skillet.
2. Pour off grease.
3. Add onions, stir until tender.
4. Add: green chilis (or Rotel tomatoes), corn, tomatoes, oregano, salt, pepper.
5. Simmer for 30 minutes.

Stuffed Bell Peppers

My Uppity Woman rewarded me with this recipe as a gift.

Ingredients:

3 large bell peppers
1 cup boiling water, salted with 1 1/2 teaspoons
    salt
1/2 pound ground beef (you can use ground tur-
    key to win Dr. Joe's approval)
1 8-ounce can tomato sauce
1/2 can coarse dry bread crumbs
1 teaspoon salt
1/4 teaspoon pepper
1 tablespoon onion, minced
1 teaspoon Worcestershire sauce

Preparation:

1. Preheat oven to 350 degrees.
2. Cut a thin slice from stem end of each pepper.
3. Core and wash.
4. Cook in boiling salted water for 5 minutes.
5. Remove and drain.
6. Mix together: ground beef (or turkey), tomato sauce, bread crumbs, salt, pepper, onion, Worcestershire sauce.
7. Stuff meat mixture lightly into peppers.
8. Stand the stuffed peppers upright in a baking dish.
9. Cover and bake 45 minutes.
10. Uncover and bake 15 minutes more.

Veal with Lemon and Butter

Now I ought to admit that I am not too enthusiastic for veal, partly because it is what it is. Still, some of you think veal is better than cold watermelon on the Fourth of July, so for you, here is a simple enough recipe. By saying "simple" I do not mean to insult your intelligence, taste, or skill: we HouseHusbands need to hang together! What I mean, I suppose, is "quick."

Ingredients:

1 pound of veal, quartered
4 tablespoons unsalted butter
Flour
Freshly ground pepper
Salt
Lemon juice

Preparation:

1. Pound veal slices with meat mallet.
2. Sprinkle them with salt and pepper.
3. Flour them.
4. Melt the butter in a large frying pan.
5. Brown the veal quickly.
6. Drizzle a little lemon juice over the meat.
7. Cook another 2 minutes, or until meat is done to your taste.

Barbecued Chicken

Now we are into chicken. After a visit to Dr. Joe, you get to eat a lot of this stuff. The trick is to sneak up on chicken with sauces and things so you don't have a dish that tastes the same all the time, even if you know in your heart that it is the same thing.

Even husbands barbecue, but they always do it outdoors. This gives them the Campfire Mystique and makes them feel as if this method is more, well, manly. It isn't.

Ingredients:

2 to 3 pounds chicken pieces, mixed, or just the pieces you want. They can be purchased separately at any supermarket. Skin them.
2/3 cup Pioneer or Bisquick baking mix
1 1/2 teaspoon paprika
1 1/4 teaspoon salt
1/4 teaspoon pepper

Preparation:

1. Start barbecue briquettes. If you have an outdoor, natural gas grill, you can wait to light it when ready to use.
2. Mix: paprika, salt, pepper, baking mix.
3. Remove skin from chicken.
4. Coat chicken with mixture from Step 2.
5. Place on grill and cook 20 to 30 minutes.
6. Turn and cook until tender.

As an alternate, or additional step, coat chicken with your favorite commercial barbecue sauce in step 4.

Bride's Chicken

Time was, brides were not Uppity. Now, most of them are that way even before they get married. One of them may have even given you this book as a wedding gift so you will understand how the game is to be played after the honeymoon. Why don't they call this "Groom's Chicken?" Because that would be redundant. This one still tastes like chicken, so read on.

Ingredients:

1/2 cup uncooked rice
1 cup water
2 pounds chicken, cut up
1/2 teaspoon salt
1/2 envelope dry onion soup mix

Preparation:

1. Combine in a baking dish: rice, water.
2. Add: chicken, salt.
3. Sprinkle with onion soup mix.
4. Cover lightly with aluminum foil.
5. Bake at 400 degrees for 1 hour.
6. Add water if needed.

Broiled Chicken

Now this is where I use the barbecue sauce a lot, because this one really tastes like chicken unless you pour on the sauce. In fact, use a lot of sauce. This simple recipe makes a good meat dish for those days when you have worked hard at the office.

Ingredients:

4 chicken breasts, skinned and boned
1/4 cup olive oil
1/2 teaspoon garlic powder
Black pepper, freshly ground, to taste
Salt, to taste

Preparation:

1. Blend together in a cup: oil, garlic powder, salt, pepper.
2. Place the chicken breasts in a lightly oiled pan.
3. Brush both sides of the chicken with oil mixture.
4. Place under broiler for 10 minutes.
5. Turn chicken over.
6. Brush chicken with the oil mixture.
7. Broil for 10 minutes.
8. Repeat this process one more time.
9. Serve chicken on warm plates.

Chicken a la Can Can

Maybe this should be Chicken Can Can Can, because you use 3 cans of something. Even the French must have their kicks.

Ingredients:

1 can cream of chicken soup
1 can cream of celery soup
1 can chicken, boned (they usually don't put the skin in canned chickens)
1 cup minute rice, cooked
1 cup water
1 can french fried onions

Preparation:

1. Combine and boil together all of the above, except french fried onions, for 5 minutes.
2. Put in a greased casserole dish.
3. Top with one can of french fried onions.
4. Bake at 350 degrees for 20 minutes.

Chicken and Spaghetti

This one makes a lot, so again it will feed a bunch if unexpected folks show up for dinner. Besides, it is better the next day (an old HouseHusband's tale to justify frugality), and can be warmed in the Microwave easily.

Ingredients:

1 package long spaghetti
1 chicken, skinned
1 small jar pimento
1/2 onion, chopped
1 cup celery, chopped
1 can cream of mushroom soup
1 can tomato soup
1 tablespoon Worcestershire sauce
1 small box Velveeta cheese, chopped finely
Ripe olives, diced (if desired)

Preparation:

1. Cook chicken until tender.
2. Bone chicken.
3. Cook spaghetti in chicken broth.
4. In another pan sauté onion and celery.
5. Drain spaghetti.
6. Mix together: chicken, spaghetti, onion, celery.
7. Add: pimento, Worcestershire sauce, cream of mushroom soup, tomato soup, cheese, olives.
8. Salt and pepper to taste.
9. Cook for 20 minutes, simmering until cheese is melted.

Chicken Delight

This makes an excellent dish if you like the taste of tomato paste, which I do. Use enough and you won't mind the chicken at all. The flour really does help bond the paste and the bird.

Ingredients:

4 chicken breasts (or other parts), skinned
Salt
Flour
1 can tomato paste
1 onion chopped
1 tablespoon Worcestershire sauce
1/2 to 1 cup water

Preparation:

1. Remove all fat and/or skin from chicken parts. Thighs or drumsticks may be used with breasts.
2. Chop onion.
3. Combine onion, tomato paste, Worcestershire sauce, and water, mixing into a batter-like consistency.
4. Salt chicken parts.
5. Place chicken in a 9 x 13 x 2 inch baking dish.
6. Sprinkle chicken with flour.
7. Pour sauce-batter over chicken, evenly, save some.
8. Bake at 350 degrees about 1 hour and 10 to 15 minutes. Check after 30 minutes to see if chicken is dry. If so, pour remaining sauce-batter over it.

Chicken Enchiladas

Our Mexican friends have long specialized in chicken enchiladas, so you probably have eaten them before. This recipe isn't too hard, so give it a try if you are hungry for Mexican food.

Ingredients:

1 whole chicken, skinned
1/2 cup chicken broth
1 tablespoon flour
1/2 pound Monterey Jack cheese
2 teaspoons salt
1 pint sour cream
1 pint whipping cream
2 tablespoons onion, grated
1 package chicken taco mix
Corn tortillas

Preparation:
1. Boil chicken and remove meat from bones.
2. Chop meat into small pieces, place in large bowl.
3. Stir taco mix and 1/2 cup broth together.
4. As you stir, gradually add: sour cream, whipping cream, onion, salt.
5. Heat until bubbly and keep warm.
6. Dip tortillas in sauce, place on cutting board or wax paper.
7. Put some chopped chicken in the middle of the wet tortilla and sprinkle with cheese.
8. Roll the tortilla around the chicken tightly.
9. Place in a 9 x 13 x 2 inch baking dish.
10. Repeat until you run out of chicken or tortillas.
11. Pour remaining sauce over the enchiladas.
12. Bake at 350 degrees for 30 minutes.

Chicken N' Rice

This dish is a good one to start with, because it really does taste like chicken.

Ingredients:

**4 chicken breasts and other parts, if desired,
  skinned
1 1/2 cups uncooked rice
2 cups water or canned chicken broth
1 teaspoon salt
1 tablespoon margarine**

Preparation:

1. Remove fat and/or skin from chicken parts.
2. Place uncooked rice evenly in a 9 x 13 x 2 inch baking dish.
3. Add salt.
4. Add margarine.
5. Add water or chicken broth.
6. Spread evenly in dish.
7. Place chicken parts in dish.
8. Bake at 350 degrees about 1 hour and 5 to 10 minutes, covered with aluminum foil.
9. Check to see when rice and chicken are done. Chicken should be white all the way through when pricked with a fork.

Chicken With Sherry

At least this one tastes more like burnt cork, especially if you are more generous with the sherry and hold back a little on the cream of chicken soup.

I really don't know where I got all these chicken recipes. Some of them were given to me by friends and students, some came from the newspaper, and some I just made up. So the odds are three to one that I got them from there. Another Yogi Berraism.

Ingredients:

8 to 10 pieces chicken (breast and thighs), skinned
Salt and pepper
1/2 cup sherry
1 can cream of celery soup
1 can cream of chicken soup

Preparation:

1. Arrange chicken in a large glass baking dish.
2. Salt and pepper to taste.
3. In a pan mix and heat together: sherry, cream of celery soup, cream of chicken soup.
4. Bring to a boil.
5. Pour over chicken.
6. Bake uncovered at 325 degrees until chicken is done. Check after about 1 hour and 15 minutes.

Company Chicken

More chicken. Keep going. We'll get to fish by and by. This one is called "Company Chicken," I suppose, because it is pretty, so you may want to serve it when "company" comes.

Ingredients:

1 1/2 cups chicken, cubed, skinned
2 teaspoons cooking oil
1 cup water
1 tablespoon dry sherry wine
1 package frozen broccoli
1 can cream of chicken soup
1 1/3 cups minute rice
1 tablespoon Parmesan cheese, grated

Preparation:

1. Place cooking oil in pan and lightly brown chicken.
2. Add: water, wine, broccoli, cream of chicken soup.
3. Bring to a full boil.
4. Separate broccoli pieces as it cooks.
5. Stir in rice.
6. Cover, cook until chicken is tender and remove from heat and let stand for 5 minutes.

Crispy Baked Chicken

No, the corn flakes do not make this a breakfast dish. It is another way to use chicken that camouflages it a little.

Ingredients:

2 to 3-pound fryer, cut up and skinned
1 cup corn flake crumbs
1 cup milk
Salt and pepper to taste

Preparation:

1. Preheat oven to 400 degrees.
2. Rinse and dry chicken pieces thoroughly.
3. Season with salt and pepper.
4. Dip each piece of chicken into milk.
5. Shake to reduce excess.
6. Roll in corn flake crumbs.
7. Let stand a few minutes so crumbs will stick.
8. Place pieces of chicken into a greased baking pan, being sure they do not touch.
9. Bake for 45 minutes.

Curry Chicken

I wish I could say I got this recipe from an Old Indian or that this offers something good to know how to prepare when next you visit Delhi. You are more likely to find Curry Chicken in an American deli, or be told it is deli-cious, if you make it right. Better go easy on the curry, unless you already know you like it.

Ingredients:

8 chicken breasts
2 packages frozen broccoli
1 can cream of chicken soup
1/2 cup mayonnaise
1 tablespoon lemon juice
3 tablespoons curry powder
1 cup grated cheddar cheese
1/2 cup water
Bread crumbs

Preparation:

1. Boil chicken until cooked, about 45 minutes.
2. When chicken cools, remove meat from bones. This is easier done with fingers than with a knife.
3. Prepare broccoli as directed on package.
4. Cover bottom of a 9 x 13 x 2 inch baking dish with a layer of broccoli.
5. Add a layer of chicken.
6. Mix: cream of chicken soup, mayonnaise, lemon juice, curry powder, water.
7. Pour over chicken.
8. Place grated cheese and bread crumbs on top.
9. Bake at 375 degrees for 25 minutes, or until cheese begins to brown.

Greek Chicken

Notice that I always skin the chicken. Probably the Greeks don't go to that much trouble. Though I have often been in hot grease, I have never been to Greece, so I really don't know, or care. I am not going to eat that slippery skin in Athens or in Texas. Use enough oregano.

Ingredients:

4 chicken breasts, skinned
1 1/2 cups lemon juice
1 cup water, hot
6 chicken bouillon cubes
3 tablespoons olive oil
1 tablespoon oregano
1 tablespoon garlic powder

Preparation:

1. Place chicken breasts in a 9 x 13 x 2 inch baking dish.
2. Mix together: lemon juice, water, chicken bouillon cubes, olive oil, oregano, garlic powder.
3. Mix until cubes dissolve.
4. Pour mixture over chicken.
5. Bake at 350 degrees for 1 1/2 hours or until chicken is cooked through.
6. Retain juice as a dip for chicken if desired.

Hot Chicken Salad

By now you must have accumulated a lot of unused chicken. This is something you can do with it.

Ingredients:

2 cups cooked, boned, and skinned chicken
1 can cream of chicken soup
2 cups celery, chopped
1/2 cup toasted almonds, chopped
1 teaspoon salt
1/4 teaspoon pepper, or to taste
1 tablespoon lemon juice
1/2 cup mayonnaise
3 hard boiled eggs, chopped
1/2 cup onion, chopped
1 cup crushed potato chips

Preparation:

1. Boil 3 to 4 chicken breasts until done. Meat will be white and tender.
2. Mix: chicken, cream of chicken soup, celery, almonds, salt, pepper, lemon juice, mayonnaise, eggs, onion.
3. Pour mixture into 9 x 13 x 2 inch baking dish.
4. Sprinkle potato chips on top.
5. Bake at 450 degrees for 15 minutes. Remove while celery and almonds are still crisp.

Mexican Chicken Casserole

You knew sooner or later I would get chicken into a Mexican dish, didn't you? I have seen this called King Ranch Casserole, but I don't know why. I thought the King Ranch raised beef and horses. Maybe when they get tired of eating beef and riding horses, the vaqueros eat chicken.

Ingredients:

4 chicken breasts
1 teaspoon salt, or to taste
1 teaspoon pepper, or to taste
1 teaspoon Seasonall
1 can cream of chicken soup
1 can cream of mushroom soup
1 can tomatoes with chilis
1 cup chicken broth
12 corn tortillas, torn into small pieces
2 onions, chopped
3 cups grated cheddar cheese

Preparation:

1. Cook chicken in water with salt and pepper until tender.
2. Cut chicken into bite size pieces.
3. Combine and mix well: cream of chicken soup, cream of mushroom soup, tomatoes, chicken broth, chopped onions.
4. Layer in two 9 x 13 x 2 baking dishes as follows: soup mixture from step 3 above, tortilla pieces, chicken, cheese.
5. Repeat, making sure cheese is on top.
6. Bake at 350 degrees for 45 minutes to 1 hour.

Sour Cream Chicken Breasts

You may note here that I usually use chicken breasts instead of the other parts. Mostly that is because you can buy them cut that way, and the nice butcher has removed the skin already, a distasteful and sometimes dangerous task. Chicken is greasy, you see, and difficult to hold. If your hand slips into a sharp knife, you may have to go out to dinner until your wound heals.

Ingredients:

4 chicken breasts, skinned
1 3-ounce can mushrooms
1 can cream of mushroom soup
1 small can evaporated milk
1 pint sour cream
Paprika

Preparation:

1. Place chicken breasts in a 9 x 13 x 2 inch baking dish.
2. Place mushrooms evenly over chicken.
3. Combine sour cream, mushroom soup, and milk.
4. Pour over chicken.
5. Dust with paprika.
6. Bake at 350 degrees for 1 hour and 30 minutes.

Beans and Sausage Dinner

This is an old bachelor evergreen. Even young boys can do this one.

Ingredients:

2 pounds dry pinto beans
2 pounds sausage (you can get this in turkey too,
      and you still can't tell the difference)
1 large purple onion
2 cloves garlic
1 teaspoon garlic salt
2 jalapeño peppers, chopped (optional)
6 to 8 cups of water

Preparation:

1. Place beans in a slow cooker or Crock Pot in early morning.
2. Add 6 to 8 cups of water.
3. Cut sausage in 1/2-inch lengths and add to pot.
4. Add: onion, garlic, garlic salt, peppers.
5. Stir thoroughly.
6. Cover and cook all day.
7. May be served with white or brown rice.

Sausage-Bean Chowder

This one is more difficult but worth the extra effort. Don't worry about the onions and garlic: it is difficult to get too much of these superb ingredients. Of course, if your Uppity Woman faces a heavy afternoon of meetings, use this one for dinner instead of lunch.

Ingredients:

1 pound bulk pork sausage (links, Polish, other kinds, and remember sausage can be made from turkey)
2 cans (16-ounce each) kidney beans
1 can (1 pound, 13-ounce) tomatoes broken up
1 quart water
1/2 bell pepper, chopped
1 large onion, chopped
1 bay leaf
1 1/2 teaspoons seasoned salt
1/2 teaspoon garlic salt
1/2 teaspoon thyme
1 cup diced potatoes (more if you wish)
1/8 teaspoon pepper

Preparation:

1. In a skillet, cook sausage until done.
2. Pour off grease.
3. In a large kettle, combine: beans, tomatoes, water, onion, bay leaf, seasoned salt, garlic salt, thyme, pepper.
4. Add sausage.
5. Simmer covered, 1 hour.
6. Add potatoes and bell pepper.
7. Cook covered 15 to 20 minutes, until potatoes are tender.
8. Remove bay leaf.

Yield: 8 generous portions. (It's even better left over, and it freezes well.)

Spanish Pork Chops

Pork chops, sometimes advertised these days as "the other white meat," taste good and are filling. This might be a good bet when you take a notion for pork. I would have said "pig," but such words are best not used when Uppity Women are around unless they say it themselves.

Ingredients:

6 lean pork chops
3/4 cups uncooked rice
1 8-ounce can tomato juice or sauce
1 teaspoon salt
1 onion, chopped
1 bell pepper, chopped
1 cup water

Preparation:

1. Trim fat and bone from pork chops.
2. Place pork chops in an iron skillet.
3. Place rice over pork chops.
4. Sprinkle with salt.
5. Sprinkle with pepper.
6. Add onions.
7. Add bell pepper.
8. Mix tomato juice or sauce and water.
9. Pour mixture over all ingredients.
10. Stir to even texture.
11. Cover and bake at 350 degrees for 45 minutes to 1 hour or until pork chops and rice are done.
12. Check to see if more water is needed during baking to prevent from becoming too dry.

Baked White Fish

When you come off fried food, this is a good way to prepare fish. The shrimp are relatively high in cholesterol, but low in fat, according to the latest thing I read in the newspaper. You might like to serve the baked fish over rice. This makes a "pretty dish" in case the Uppity Woman is bringing home a guest. This recipe came from my friend Valentine J. Belfiglio, and I added a few touches of my own.

Ingredients:

4 fish fillets
1 can small cocktail shrimp
1 can crabmeat
1/2 onion, minced
1/2 bell pepper, minced
2 tablespoons olive oil
1/4 teaspoon oregano
Freshly ground pepper, to taste
1 tablespoon pimento
Bread crumbs
Salt, to taste

Preparation:

1. Place fish fillets into a baking dish.
2. Drizzle the oil over the fish.
3. Mix together: shrimp, crabmeat, onion, bread crumbs, pimento.
4. Spread over the fish.
5. Bake in preheated oven at 350 degrees for 40 minutes.

Boiled Shrimp

Now shrimps are not far behind 'dem crawfish when it comes to good eatin'. You can do anything to a shrimp you want, but you can't beat the simplest way to eat them: boiled. Eating must be done with the hands. I don't know why, but when someone peels shrimp for you and then provides a little three-pronged cocktail fork to shovel the shrimp to your mouth, you lose somethin' in the transition. Remember to be wary of the real French, who invented the fork. Cajuns, even us adopted ones, know that the fingers are the proper tools for delivering the shrimps to the mouth.

Ingredients:

2 pounds shrimp (or as many as you want), de-headed but with shells
3 tablespoons liquid crab and shrimp boil spices
1 tablespoon cayenne pepper, or to taste
2 tablespoons lemon juice

Preparation:

1. Using large pot, fill with at least a gallon of water.
2. Add crab and shrimp boil.
3. Add cayenne pepper.
4. Add lemon juice.
5. Bring to a boil.
6. Add shrimp.
7. Cook uncovered for 5 minutes
8. Peel shell and taste a shrimp to see if done. If not, cook 2 minutes and test again.
9. Drain shrimp in colander.
10. Serve immediately or refrigerate and serve later. Good either way.

11. Give each person a cup, towel, and platter for shells.
12. Peel shells before eating.
13. Dip in cocktail sauce or catsup.

Accompanies: French Fried Potatoes, Green Salad

Crawfish Etouffée

At last a REAL Cajun entry. "Cajun" is a corruption of the word "Acadian," but there is nothing corrupting about their food, except that it is addictive. After having "passed a few years" in "Bat-Ton Rouge," and visiting my mother and dad in Lake Charles, I am an authority on Cajun cooking. I can't cook Cajun very well, but I am an authority on it nonetheless. I certify that when Cajun cooking is done well, there is none better. So we start with the crawfish, properly pronounced, "cRAWfish," the national animal of Acadiana.

Ingredients:

2 pounds peeled crawfish tails
1 cup green onions with tops
1 cup chopped celery
1/2 cup chopped bell peppers
1/2 cup cooking oil
1 can Rotel tomatoes
1 can tomato sauce
1/2 cup chopped parsley
2 teaspoons cornstarch
1 teaspoon salt
1 teaspoon pepper, or to taste

Preparation:

1. Pour oil in a large pot.
2. Sauté: onions, celery, bell peppers.
3. When all are tender, add: Rotel tomatoes, tomato sauce, parsley, cornstarch, salt, pepper.
4. Simmer for one hour.
5. Add crawfish tails.
6. Cook until crawfish are tender.
7. Serve over cooked rice, page 130.

Salmon Patties

There is not much that will redeem this dish for the low-cholesterol crowd because of the frying, but it is a tasty dish. I suppose you could peel the crust and just eat the salmon, but that hardly seems fair since you have gone to the trouble to fry the patties. Maybe if you like salmon patties, you can sneak this in once in a while if you are good the rest of the week. This one brings back memories; canned salmon prepared this way was a standard on my mother's table, so for nostalgia, if nothing else, I include this one.

Ingredients:

1 can salmon
2 1/2 cups mashed potatoes
1 egg, well-beaten
2 tablespoons flour
1/2 cup onions, chopped
Salt and pepper
Cooking oil

Preparation:

1. Mix together well: salmon, mashed potatoes, egg, flour, onion, salt and pepper.
2. Shape into patties.
3. Roll the patties in flour.
4. Fry in deep oil until golden brown.

Hazel's Venison Roast

Hazel is the former Hazel Shelton, who somehow got mixed up with that Abernethy boy. They've stayed married until now, raised five kids, and are both accomplished in their chosen fields. One of Ab's interests is hunting, especially deer, as is often the case with Southern men. Since Ab is such a good provider of game, Hazel has to devise ways to use it all. Her recipe for venison roast is so good you will think it tastes like beef. If you want the gamey taste, you are out of luck. You must provide your own venison. At current costs for guns, ammunition, hunting license, and other items, venison costs about $50 a pound. But there is no greater thrill for a HouseHusband than cooking the produce of his garden or his hunting trip.

Ingredients:

1 venison roast
1 package dry Lipton Onion Soup Mix
1 can Cream of Mushroom Soup (no water)
Worcestershire sauce to taste
1 cup or so of red wine
Meat tenderizer

Preparation:

1. Line pan generously with foil, leaving enough to seal meat later.
2. Sprinkle meat tenderizer on roast.
3. Spread Cream of Mushroom Soup on roast.
4. Spread Lipton Dry Onion Soup Mix on roast.
5. Add red wine and 1/2 to 1 cup of water to keep meat from tasting "dry."
6. Fold over foil and seal.
7. Bake at 350 degrees for about 2 hours.

2

Vegetables

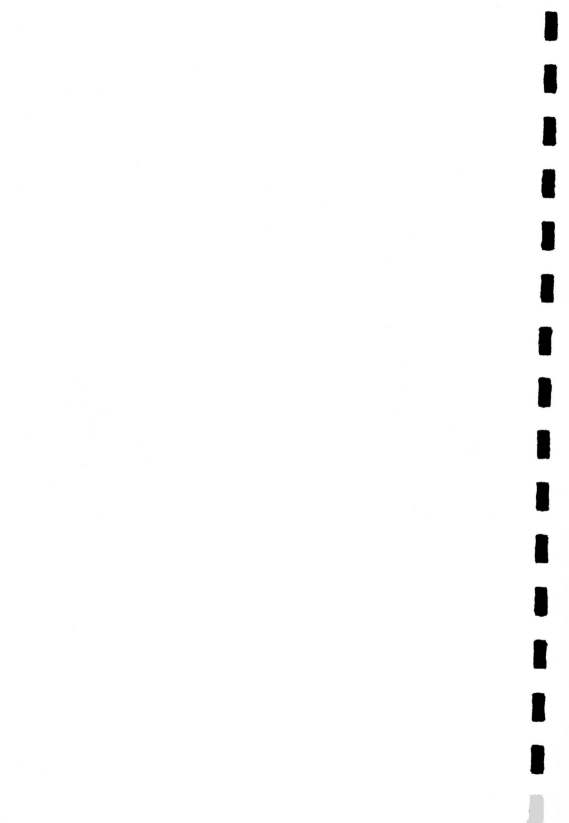

Traditionally, most men are meat eaters. According to some psychologists, this carnivorous activity makes them aggressive, assertive, and masculine. Would it necessarily follow that when a woman manifests symptoms of Uppityness, that she is eating too much meat? Of course not. Whether one enjoys the flesh of animals is not a matter of gender, but of taste. One of the most extreme cases of male wimpishness in my acquaintance will eat meat and little else.

On the other hand, you have vegetarians. They come in two varieties: Purists, who will eat only plant products, even denying themselves milk and eggs; the Less-Than-Pure-But-Still-Holier-Than-Others, who claim to be vegetarians but put cheese sauce on their broccoli.

The Greeks had all this scoped out thousands of years ago. They called their solution the Golden Mean. Most modern folks simply phrase this as "everything in moderation." What I really want to do here is say to those who worry about their meat vs. vegetable consumption, is that it is all right to enjoy vegetables. Of all the things you eat, vegetables probably are the best for you if you eat a variety of the green and yellow ones, and do not concentrate exclusively on one or the other. This statement is not based on scientific study, for I am a person of the liberal arts; rather, it is based on what my Aunt Jonnie, who loved to frighten me, told me years ago.

Aunt Jonnie said that if I ate only one color vegetable that I would eventually turn that color. Now I didn't want to turn green, or yellow either for that matter, so I developed early the habit of consuming a variety of vegetables. I have to give credit to my Uppity Woman for development of an even broader appreciation of vegetables.

This development came, of course, in the days before she was uppity and still did the cooking. She would sneak onions into things and, once cooked, the onions mostly disappeared so you couldn't see them and sometimes couldn't even taste them, at least not the way they tasted when eaten raw.

Now onions are a vital part of nearly everything I prepare. She never did bring me around to brussel sprouts, and I haven't come to terms with eggplant, but my horizons are broadening. I have no prejudice against eggplant, I just can't quite figure out what to do with one.

The Bottom Line, as they say in business, is that the House-Husband must deal with vegetables. Long before the introduction of HouseHusbandry, most married men, and even show-off singles, enjoyed going forth into the backyard to barbecue. While that work has a specific meaning in food preparation, it has become a euphemism for any kind of meat preparation done outdoors.

Men "bar-be-qued" and depended on the Little Woman to prepare a salad, baked potato, and other meal contributions in the kitchen. All that is over. Now that you have the full responsibility for a meal that must be served on schedule that will enable the Uppity Woman to make a 7 p.m. meeting, you must prepare the meat and the vegetables simultaneously. I used to call this "Making it come out even," and it is no easy thing to do. One dish was always ready before another, some were over-cooked, and some could have benefited from a few more minutes contact with the oven or the cooktop. But practice improves things, so that in time they come out pretty well "even."

Now back to vegetables. Once you get the hang of preparing them, they are not that much more trouble than what you formerly did in the backyard. I always prefer to use fresh vegetables, and of course the freshest come from your own garden, but that is another book. If you do not already have a garden, do not stop to learn how now. You will starve to death or be condemned to eating in restaurants all the time. Take one thing at a time.

If you do not garden, at least purchase fresh vegetables from the produce department of your supermarket. Sometimes roadside bargains can be realized at vegetable stands, but usually such purchases are as expensive as what you can buy in the grocery store. Ask the produce manager for help in selecting the freshest vegetables. He will be grateful for the conversation since most people treat him as part of the store's fixtures.

If fresh vegetables are not in season, frozen vegetables are the next most desirable, followed by canned vegetables. The newspaper tells me there is not much nutritional difference between them, but now that you are in charge of the kitchen, do you want to look like you are no more than an opener of cans? Of course not! You want it known that you *cooked* the meal, not just warmed the contents of a can.

Consider the following ways to cook vegetables. If you just must have meat, you can cook that, too. Even in the backyard.

112

Potato Pancakes

The potato is a versatile vegetable. You can bake, fry, or boil them — and even grate them. Best of all you can eat them. They are low in calories and you don't have to worry about fat. Of course, most folks doctor them up with so much cheese, bacon, sour cream, and/or butter that the poor potato is lost somewhere in the process. This is a good way to make them a little different.

Ingredients:

6 medium potatoes, peeled and grated
1 small onion, finely chopped
3 eggs
3/4 cup flour
2 teaspoons salt
Oil sufficient to fry

Preparation:

1. Fill a bowl halfway with cold water.
2. Grate potatoes, on coarse side of grater, into bowl of cold water.
3. In separate bowl, combine for the batter: onion, eggs, flour, salt.
4. Drain potatoes.
5. Beat potatoes into batter.
6. Spoon portions of batter into hot oil, mash into 3- to 4-inch patties.
7. Brown on one side, then turn with spatula.
8. Brown second side.
9. Cook fairly slowly so potatoes will cook thoroughly.
10. Drain a few seconds on paper towel before serving.

Stuffed Baked Potatoes

There is nothing especially original about a stuffed potato. Most restaurants prepare these as a matter of course, and there are Potato Bars that provide even more ingredients for you to inflict upon the potato. I have to confess that I prefer the potato with just salt and pepper, and perhaps a little margarine or liquid Butter-Buds. However, I do admit that a Stuffed Potato is much prettier. When you are scraping the thing out, be careful not to penetrate all the way to the skin. If you do, your stuffing will run out.

Ingredients:

4 large baking potatoes
1 cup hot milk
3 to 4 drops Worcestershire sauce
1/2 teaspoon mustard
1/4 teaspoon black pepper
2 tablespoons parsley chopped
1 cup grated cheddar cheese
1 teaspoon salt
Paprika

Preparation:

1. Wash potatoes thoroughly.
2. Bake potatoes, if possible, in a microwave oven. Pierce each potato with a fork. Cook on High setting, allowing about 5 to 6 minutes per potato, or for 20 to 25 minutes total. May be baked in oven at 400 degrees for 1 hour, if you don't have a microwave.
3. Remove potatoes and cut lengthwise in halves.
4. Scrape potato out of skin into a bowl and save skins for stuffing later.

5. Add milk to potatoes.
6. Whip until fluffy.
7. Add: Worcestershire sauce, mustard, salt, pepper, parsley.
8. Stir.
9. Heap mixture into potato skins.
10. Sprinkle cheese and paprika on top.
11. Bake at 350 degrees for 10 to 15 minutes.

Sidney's Potatoes

My friend Sidney Abegg is a Chamber of Commerce director who fancies himself a cook. He makes excellent gumbo, and when he sets his mind to it he can do other things well. What he mostly wants to do is barbecue. It is as if the world's supply of steak is running out and he wants to get his share. He likes pizza, too. Sidney's credentials as a HouseHusband are substantiated mostly by the Uppityness of his wife, Marilyn, and his ability to make Sidney's Potatoes. It is a good dish that will go with just about anything.

Ingredients:

6 to 7 potatoes, peeled and cut into chunks (about 1/4-inch thick and one-inch square)
1 onion cut into small chunks
3/4 stick margarine
Mrs. Dash seasoning
1 cup white wine

Preparation:

1. Peel potatoes.
2. Cut onions.
3. Cut potatoes.
4. Layer potatoes in pyrex or comparable baking dish.
5. Layer onions.
6. Repeat layers.
7. Cut 1/4-inch-thick slices of margarine, spread on top.
8. Sprinkle Mrs. Dash seasoning generously over layers.
9. Add 1 cup wine.

10. Bake uncovered at 325 degrees for 1 hour and 15 minutes or until potatoes are soft and onions clear.
11. After baking 30 minutes, stir thoroughly to moisten top layers, add 1/4 cup wine, if necessary, to keep moist.
12. After baking 1 hour, stir again to keep vegetables from sticking to sides and bottom, and if necessary, add more margarine or wine (or water).

Scalloped Potatoes

What this mostly does is add cheese to Sidney's Potatoes. If you are a cheese advocate, here is a good way to work it in.

Ingredients:

6 to 8 potatoes, cut in chunks about 1/4-inch
thick and one-inch square
1/4 to 1/2 pound American or cheddar cheese,
shredded
1 green pepper cut in small pieces
1 onion diced
3/4 stick margarine
Salt to taste or Mrs. Dash seasoning to taste
1 small can pimiento
1 cup milk

Preparation:

1. Mix ingredients in buttered 9 x 13 x 2 baking dish.
2. Bake uncovered 45 minutes to 1 hour and 15 minutes, at 350 degrees, checking to see when potatoes are done.

Easy Scalloped Potatoes

Anything advertised as "easy" usually isn't. I don't see much difference in this and ordinary scalloped potatoes except when you add the cheese. If that makes things easier, by all means do it.

Ingredients:

6 to 8 medium potatoes peeled and thinly sliced
1 medium onion, thinly sliced
1 can cream of mushroom soup
1 cup milk
2 tablespoons margarine
Salt and pepper to taste
1 cup of your favorite cheese, grated

Preparation:

1. Layer potatoes and onions in a well-greased casserole dish.
2. Season each layer with the salt and pepper.
3. Blend the milk and soup together.
4. Pour over the layered casserole.
5. Dot with margarine.
6. Bake covered at 350 degrees for 1 hour.
7. During the last 15 minutes of baking, remove cover and sprinkle with cheese.

New Potatoes
(or Small Peeled Irish Potatoes)

New potatoes are the (usually) smaller reddish potatoes. They do have a different flavor than Irish potatoes, and are especially good when served with green beans. You can even cook them together if you wish.

Ingredients:

8 to 10 new potatoes
1 tablespoon bacon drippings or a couple of bacon slices (the low cholesterol crowd can use ButterBuds instead)
1 teaspoon salt
Black pepper to taste

Preparation:

1. Wash potatoes thoroughly. If using new potatoes, remove the thin, outer red skin with water and a stiff brush. Leave inner skin. If using Irish potatoes, you may want to remove peeling.
2. Place in pot with water sufficient to cover.
3. Add: bacon drippings (or bacon or ButterBuds), salt.
4. Cover and cook on High setting until water begins to boil.
5. Reduce heat to Low and cook about 30 minutes, or until a fork easily pierces potato to the center.
6. Drain and place in a serving dish and sprinkle with black pepper.

May be eaten with butter (or liquid ButterBuds) if desired.

Prepare Ahead Potato-Cheese Casserole

This one is good when you know ahead of time that you have to have a meal prepared but will not have enough time to do it after you get off work. Of course you will serve more than potatoes, unless you are especially fond of them and can make an entire meal of one dish. If you have a pre-battered turkey or beef patty, you can put that in the oven as well and make a salad while the rest of the dinner prepares itself in the oven.

Ingredients:

6 large potatoes, boiled with the peel on
2 cups sour cream
2 cups American cheddar cheese, grated
3 green onions, chopped, including tops
1 stick margarine
2 teaspoons salt
Pepper to taste

Preparation:

1. Cook and peel potatoes.
2. Grate coarsely, or cube potatoes.
3. Mix together: potatoes, sour cream, 1 cup cheddar cheese, green onions, margarine, salt, pepper.
4. Place in casserole dish and refrigerate until ready to use.
5. When ready to serve, remove from refrigerator.
6. Sprinkle 1 cup cheddar cheese over top of casserole.
7. Cover and bake in oven at 350 degrees for 35 minutes.

Bourbon Sweet Potatoes

This is a great winter casserole, especially appropriate for Thanksgiving or Christmas dinner. It is nice with pork dishes, too.

Ingredients:

6 medium sweet potatoes
1/2 cup sugar
1 teaspoon salt
3/4 stick butter or margarine
Nutmeg, dash
1 egg, beaten
1/2 cup bourbon whiskey
Marshmallows for topping

Preparation:

1. Boil sweet potatoes until fork tender.
2. When cooked, peel and mash potatoes.
3. Add: sugar, salt, butter or margarine, nutmeg.
4. Beat egg into whiskey.
5. Mix in potato mixture.
6. Place in a pyrex baking dish and top with marshmallow halves.
7. Bake in a 350 degrees oven for 45 minutes or until marshmallows are golden brown.

Broiled Tomatoes

Despite what I said earlier about tomatoes, they are versatile, too. These recipes for broiled and baked tomatoes are the simplest ways to serve them. I prefer the second, or the one for baked tomato. It is quite easy to do, and almost impossible to mess up unless you leave the tomatoes in the oven too long. Tomato adds color to the plate, and can accompany any meat dish you serve.

Ingredients:

2 tomatoes, halved
Salt and pepper, to taste
1 scant cup sour cream
Paprika to garnish

Preparation:

1. Place tomato halves in Pyrex baking dish.
2. Salt and pepper to taste.
3. Cover each tomato half with a generous portion of sour cream.
4. Sprinkle with paprika.
5. Place under slow broiler and cook until sides of tomatoes are soft and sour cream turns golden brown.

Baked Tomatoes

Ingredients:

Tomatoes
Mozzarella cheese
Parmesan cheese
Salt and pepper, to taste

Preparation:

1. Cut as many tomatoes as you want into halves.
2. Sprinkle salt, then pepper on each half.
3. Add mozzarella cheese and Parmesan to cover top.
4. Bake about 10 to 12 minutes, or until tomato is warm and cheese has melted.

Okra and Tomatoes

This is a standard at our house. I would like to call it Southern because okra seems to me to be a Southern plant. This is a combination that is better than its constituent parts if eaten separately. Many find boiled okra too slimy, and fried okra, though tasty, is, after all, fried. Tomatoes are best eaten within two seconds after they come off the vine when they are still warm from the sun. You can never find them that way unless you grow them yourself. But even store-bought tomatoes take on a new flavor when combined with okra this way. Be careful with the pepper; most Uppity Women don't like too much.

Ingredients:

1 1/2 pounds okra
1 pound fresh tomatoes
1 teaspoon salt
Pepper
3 slices of bacon (or 1 package of ButterBuds)
Onion, chopped if you like it, as much as you
**   want**

Preparation:

1. Cut okra into pieces 1/4 to 1/2 inch long.
2. Cut tomatoes into small chunks.
3. Fry bacon, remove from drippings and crumble.
4. Reduce heat to Low.
5. Place okra in hot bacon drippings, stir and turn until drippings are absorbed.
6. Cover and cook at low heat about ten minutes.
7. Add tomatoes and onions, if you use them, to okra, and stir until well mixed.
8. Add salt and sprinkle with pepper.
9. Cover and cook about 30 to 40 minutes, or until okra and tomatoes are soft and well mixed. Taste to see if done to smooth consistency.
10. Pour into serving dish and sprinkle with pepper.

Steamed Squash

You will need a steamer. You can use a retractable steamer in a larger pot. This is a quick way to use a splendid summer vegetable. And don't worry — no matter how much you eat you won't turn yellow, despite what Aunt Jonnie says.

Ingredients:

3 to 4 yellow squash
1/2 onion, sliced
Mrs. Dash seasoning

Preparation:

1. Cut squash into slices, removing small portion of stem ends.
2. Cut onion into thin slices.
3. Place steamer in pot with sufficient water just to the base of the steamer.
4. Place squash and onion in the steamer.
5. Cover and bring to a boil.
6. Reduce heat and add Mrs. Dash seasoning.
7. Cook 25 to 35 minutes, turning occasionally.
8. Taste to see if squash and onions are cooked. Squash should be soft and onions milky clear.
9. Serve and add more seasoning if desired.

Country Style Yellow Squash

Now this is the way I learned to cook squash. The bacon is mostly what you taste, so if you like the taste of bacon there is no way to dislike this dish. It is a little high in fat, though, so if that is a problem for you, you might like to stick with the steamed squash; if not, there is no better way to eat this vegetable.

Ingredients:

6 to 8 yellow squash
4 slices bacon
Salt
Pepper

Preparation:

1. Slice squash after removing small portion of stem and blossom ends.
2. Fry bacon crisp, remove to absorbent paper towel. When cool, crumble.
3. Reduce heat to Low and place squash into pan with drippings.
4. Stir until drippings are nearly absorbed.
5. Cover and cook on Low, about 10 minutes.
6. Add salt.
7. Stir, and cook about 20-30 minutes or until squash is soft.
8. Taste to see if squash is cooked to desired consistency.
9. Put in serving dish and sprinkle with black pepper and crumbled bacon.

Cherokee Squash Casserole

This casserole can be made a day ahead, but do not add bread crumbs until ready to bake. It is a wonderful casserole that complements any meal, and is a contribution from Betty Davis, who has studied the art of cooking in France. That did not ruin her, as one might expect. On the other hand, I think she knew how to do this before she went Over There.

Ingredients:

1 1/2 pound yellow squash
1 large onion, chopped
3 tablespoons bacon grease
2 cups sharp cheddar cheese, grated
1/2 stick butter or margarine
**2 tablespoons plus 2 teaspoons arrowroot or 4
     tablespoons cornstarch**
1 teaspoon salt
Cracked white pepper to taste
1 cup buttered bread crumbs

Preparation:

1. Cook together in boiling salted water until tender: squash, onion, bacon grease.
2. Drain and mash well.
3. Add while hot: grated cheese, butter or margarine.
4. Add: arrowroot (or cornstarch), salt, pepper.
5. Top with buttered bread crumbs.
6. Bake at 350 degrees for 45 minutes.

Squash Croquettes

When you look at yellow squash, you might not think of preparing it this way because this vegetable is usually served either steamed or boiled. Some people will eat anything that is fried, and this could be their only encounter with squash.

Ingredients:

2 cups finely chopped yellow squash
1 cup finely chopped onions
1 egg beaten
1 teaspoon salt
1 teaspoon pepper
1/2 cup plus 1 tablespoon all-purpose flour
Cooking oil

Preparation:

1. Combine: squash, onion, egg, salt, pepper.
2. Mix well.
3. Stir in flour.
4. Drop by tablespoonfuls into 1/2 inch of hot oil.
5. Cook until browned, turning once.
6. Drain and serve.

Rice

Rice will complement nearly anything. You can serve it in conjunction with any meat you are likely to serve; it combines well with dried beans; and leftover rice may be added to most soups. It is usually on our table on Sunday, the one day my Uppity Woman goes into the kitchen, and she usually makes a gravy to go over it. This reflects our upbringing among Cajun folk on the Texas coast.

Ingredients:

1 cup rice (serves 3 to 5 persons)
1 3/4 cup water
1 teaspoon salt
1 tablespoon margarine

Preparation:

1. Combine: rice, salt, water, margarine in a 3-quart saucepan.
2. Bring to a boil, stir.
3. Cover well, reduce heat to Low and simmer for 15 minutes.
4. Remove from heat and let stand, covered, 10 minutes longer.

Accompanies: Pinto Beans, Gravy, Butter or margarine.

You may add butter to hot rice. As it melts, stir thoroughly. Now you have "Buttered Rice" to accompany "Sour Cream Chicken Breasts."

Rice and Mushrooms

Uppity Women, and some men, like mushrooms. I don't, except in spaghetti sauce and with dried lima beans. Because most cooks work for others, you have to humor their tastes. This is a good way to show that you can use mushrooms. If you like mushrooms, so much the better.

Ingredients:

1/4 cup bell pepper, chopped
1/2 cup onion, chopped
1 tablespoon cooking oil
1 cup rice
1/4 cup parsley, chopped
2 cups beef consommé
Salt and pepper to taste
1/2 pound of fresh mushrooms, cleaned and cut
in half
2 tablespoons butter or margarine
Soy sauce to taste (2 tablespoons or 1/4 cup)

Preparation:

1. Heat oil in pan and sauté: bell pepper, onion.
2. Add: rice, parsley, consommé, salt and pepper.
3. Cover tightly and cook on Low heat on top of stove, or bake in a 350 degrees oven until rice is fluffy and liquid absorbed.
4. Melt butter or margarine in saucepan.
5. Add: lemon juice, soy sauce, mushrooms.
6. Toss mushroom halves in the warm butter mixture until they are barely cooked.
7. Combine mushroom mixture with the rice in a serving dish.
8. Garnish with chopped parsley.

Party Rice

This is a great accompaniment to a buffet or simply to enhance a meal for entertaining.

Ingredients:

**6 stalks green onions, tops and bottoms finely
      chopped
1 stick butter or margarine
2 cups rice, washed
2 tablespoons butter or margarine
4 cups boiling water
5 tablespoons soy sauce
1/2 cup slivered almonds**

Preparation:

1. Place 1 stick butter or margarine in a pan and melt.
2. Sauté green onions in the butter or margarine.
3. Place into a 2 1/2 quart pan: onions, rice, water.
4. Cover tightly and cook on Low until water has evaporated.
5. Uncover and toss rice.
6. Add: 2 tablespoons butter, soy sauce, slivered almonds.
7. Place in oven-proof casserole and warm in oven at 250 degrees for 30 minutes.

Spanish Rice

One of my sons is particularly partial to Spanish rice, and the rest of the family tolerates it, except my Uppity Woman. I don't expect that this goes with the territory when one is Uppity. Possibly your Uppity Woman will like it.

Ingredients:

1/2 pound (1 cup) rice
1 can tomato sauce
1 bell pepper, chopped
1 onion, chopped
1 can stewed tomatoes, crushed
1 teaspoon salt
1/4 teaspoon pepper, or to taste
1 teaspoon cooking oil
2 cups water

Preparation:

1. Pour oil in pan.
2. Sauté onion and pepper.
3. Add 1 cup water as you stir.
4. Add: rice, tomato sauce, stewed tomatoes, salt, pepper, 1 cup water.
5. Cover and cook 15 to 20 minutes or until rice is done.
6. Let stand covered for a few minutes before serving.

Broccoli and Rice (Green Rice)

As I said earlier, rice can be used in conjunction with many foods. In this case, the cheese really helps. You can encounter this dish a lot at covered-dish suppers, particularly at Baptist churches. You might want to use it yourself for that purpose because it is easy to prepare and does not require much time to prepare.

Ingredients:

1 box frozen chopped broccoli
1 cup rice cooked
1 can cream of mushroom soup
1 small jar Cheeze Whiz
1 onion, chopped

Preparation:

1. Cook rice. See page 130.
2. Cook broccoli, according to directions on package.
3. Mix: broccoli, rice, Cheeze Whiz, onions.
4. Pour into a greased casserole dish.
5. Bake at 350 degrees for 20 minutes.

Broccoli-Rice Casserole

This is a variation of the last recipe, but it is not much more complicated. I suppose it might be termed "Intermediate." This recipe came from Betty Davis, my friend who is a gourmet cook. Betty's husband accused her of "cooking her way through graduate school." That isn't true, but it could have been true, except she is so intelligent it didn't need to be true. She also contributed this recipe to a cookbook published by Trinity Church (Longview, Texas).

Ingredients:

1/2 stick butter or margarine
1 onion, finely chopped
1 package frozen chopped broccoli, thawed
1 can cream of mushroom soup
1 small jar Cheez Whiz
1 teaspoon Worcestershire sauce
Tabasco sauce, dash
3 cups cooked rice

Preparation:

1. Melt butter in a skillet.
2. Add onion.
3. Sauté until onion is clear.
4. Add broccoli.
5. Stir and heat through.
6. Add soup, stirring, and simmer several minutes.
7. Add Cheez Whiz, mix, and simmer a few more minutes.
8. Add: Worcestershire sauce, Tabasco sauce, rice.
9. Stir and then place in a 9-inch square casserole.
10. Bake at 350 degrees for 25 to 30 minutes.

Fresh Corn on the Cob

No garden vegetable is more dramatically different from the canned or frozen state than corn. It is important to get it from the garden to the pot as quickly as you can. Even purchased at the market, it is better than preserved corn. If garden fresh corn is available, it is by far the best.

Ingredients:

1 to 2 ears of corn per person
6 to 8 quarts water
1 teaspoon salt
Butter or margarine

Preparation:

1. Place 6 to 8 quarts water and salt into a large pan (fill it about half full) and bring to boil.
2. Shuck corn and wash to get rid of silks.
3. If an ear-worm has already enjoyed the tapered end of the cob, dispose of it and cut away the ruined portion. The remainder of the ear is still good.
4. If ears are more than four inches long, break in half if you want smaller portions.
5. Place ears in boiling water.
6. Cook uncovered for about 15 minutes.
7. Corn will turn a darker color when done.
8. Remove with kitchen tongs so corn will drain.
9. Serve with butter or margarine.

Alternative: Frozen corn on the cob, or canned corn, whole kernel or creamed. Be sure to get a quality brand. It makes a difference.

Corn Casserole

This corn casserole is another way to use one of nature's best foods. Mayans began the culture of corn in the distant past, passed it to the Europeans, and Americans embraced the culture when our ancestors arrived 500 years ago. Few Mayan women were Uppity. They understood whose duty it was to cook the corn. Well, we still know whose duty it is...but along the way from then till now, something went wrong. Oh well, enjoy the corn casserole.

Ingredients:

6 tablespoons safflower cooking oil
1 teaspoon garlic salt
2 cans cream-style corn
1 small can green chilis
2 eggs
3/4 cup corn meal
2 cups cheddar cheese, grated

Preparation:

1. Combine all of the ingredients.
2. Pour into a greased casserole baking dish.
3. Bake at 350 degrees for 1 hour.

Buttered Summer Corn

Corn offers one of the best summer vegetables to serve with any meal. In the winter, use a good quality creamed corn and it will remind you of summer.

Ingredients:

6 ears of yellow corn
1 stick of butter or margarine
1/2 cup of cream
Salt and pepper to taste
1 tablespoon sugar

Preparation:

1. Cut corn off cob, and scrape cob with sharp knife.
2. In a skillet sauté corn in the butter or margarine.
3. Add: cream, salt, pepper, sugar.
4. Cover and simmer slowly for 20 minutes, stirring occasionally.
5. If too dry, add more cream and butter.
6. Continue to cook slowly until corn is tender.

Garden Fresh Beans

If fresh garden beans are unavailable, frozen or canned beans are acceptable but they never taste as good. The green bean is a noble vegetable. It grows prolifically, and can make you lots of friends if you share them with others. I have to confess that they do taste better with the bacon, but Dr. Joe won't let me have that anymore. If that is your circumstance as well, add ButterBuds, almond slivers, and a little dill. It helps.

Ingredients:

2 to 3 pounds beans (or whatever you have)
1 tablespoon bacon drippings or a slice or two of
        uncooked bacon or ButterBuds
3/4 teaspoon salt

Preparation:

1. Snap beans by removing a small portion of each end and pulling as much "string" as possible from each side, then break beans into parts about two inches long.
2. Wash beans thoroughly.
3. Place them in a pot and add water sufficient to show among the beans.
4. Add: bacon drippings or bacon or ButterBuds, salt.
5. Cover and cook on High heat until they begin to boil.
6. Reduce heat to Low setting and cook about 30 minutes, stirring occasionally.

Accompanies: new potatoes

Green Bean Casserole

For some reason, this is the kind of food that women like. I believe if you added mushrooms to anything they would like it. Pity that mushrooms do not seem to have an aphrodisiac effect. Anyway, prepare this and serve it to her, maybe it will work anyway.

Ingredients:

2 cans cut green beans
1 can cream of mushroom soup
1 can fried onion rings

Preparation:

1. Combined green beans and cream of mushroom soup in a greased casserole dish.
2. Bake at 350 degrees for 15 minutes.
3. Add onion rings to top.
4. Bake another 5 minutes to heat onion rings.

Black "Eyes of Texas" Casserole

I cannot remember who gave me this recipe. I can't even remember preparing it. But it is here, so we may assume that it is good. At least none of the ingredients look like they will prove fatal. Drop me a line and let me know if you like it. Maybe I'll prepare it sometime.

Ingredients:

1 large can of black-eyed peas, or equal amount of
    cooked black-eyed peas
1 jalapeño pepper, chopped finely

1 1/2 pound ground beef (or turkey)
1 onion, chopped
1/4 teaspoon garlic powder
1 can tomatoes with green chilis
1 can cream of chicken soup
1 can cream of mushroom soup
1 can enchilada sauce
1/4 teaspoon hot pepper seasoning, or chili
    powder
16 corn tortillas, cut into strips
2 cups cheddar cheese, grated

Preparation:

1. Brown ground meat.
2. Pour off grease.
3. Sauté in onions and garlic.
4. Stir in: black-eyed peas, tomatoes with chilis, cream of chicken soup, cream of mushroom soup, enchilada sauce, hot pepper seasoning or chili powder.
5. Layer meat in a 9 x 13 x 2 inch baking dish.
6. Add: layer of tortilla strips, layer of meat mixture, layer of tortilla strips, layer of meat mixture.
7. Sprinkle top with cheese.
8. Bake at 350 degrees for 35 minutes or until bubbly.

Dried Lima Beans

This is a dish I learned from my mother, Pernemia Tula Tucker of Lake Charles, Louisiana. Mother isn't exactly Uppity, but she would like to be. It isn't that Daddy has a stronger hand on the reins so much as that she did not aspire to a business or political career. She still cooks a lot—and I gain weight when we go home at Christmas.

Ingredients:

1 package large lima beans, dried
2 to 4 green onions, chopped, including tops
1 ham hock (I have not found a suitable low-fat
    substitute for this)
1 can cream of mushroom soup
1/2 onion, sliced or chopped, if desired

Preparation:

1. In the morning before going to work, wash the dried lima beans thoroughly.
2. Place them in a Crock-Pot or other slow cooker.
3. Add 8 cups of water.
4. Add the ham hock.
5. Cook on High (in slow cooker) about 10 hours or until done.
6. After about 4 or 5 hours add: chopped green onions, white onion, cream of mushroom soup.
7. Stir well.
8. Before serving, taste. Hock probably will have salted beans sufficiently. If not, add salt to taste.
9. Add black pepper to taste, either in pot or individually with serving.

10. The next day a good soup can be made with leftovers. Place in blender, add water depending on how "soupy" you like bean soup, and blend. Serve with crackers, and you may want to add more pepper.

Dried Pinto Beans

These days I leave out the ham hock and, as a consequence, I don't prepare this much anymore. A little chili powder helps, but I usually use too much and my Uppity Woman doesn't like food to "burn" her mouth. If you try this one, you might want to add a teaspoon or so of dried mustard. My mother-in-law says this helps prevent the beans from giving you a gassy stomach. I don't know if it really works but I always obey my mother-in-law.

Ingredients:

1 pound pinto beans
1 ham hock
1 onion, sliced

Preparation:

1. Wash beans thoroughly.
2. Place beans in Crock-Pot.
3. Add 6 to 8 cups water.
4. Add ham hock.
5. Cook on High (in slow cooker) for about 10 hours.
6. After 4 to 5 hours stir and add onions.
7. After about 10 hours, taste. Add salt if necessary.
8. Serve alone or mixed with rice.

Fresh Garden Greens

Now here is where I show my Southern-ness. I did not intend this book to have a narrow regional appeal. After all, some Yankee women are Uppity, and some Yankee men are HouseHusbands. However, this dish probably will appeal most to Southerners. For a while, greens were known as "soul food." I can't think of a better description. Growing them, and then cooking and eating what you have grown, is truly good for the soul.

Ingredients:

1 to 2 bunches of greens (mustard, turnip, collard, chard, or beet tops)
1 tablespoon bacon drippings or 2 slices bacon or 1 package ButterBuds
1 teaspoon salt

Preparation:

1. Wash greens thoroughly. Be sure to check the underside of each leaf, to make sure it is clean.
2. If tender and fresh, whole leaves may be put into pot. You may want to remove center stems from mustard greens.
3. Add enough water to prevent sticking on bottom.
4. Add bacon drippings, bacon slices or ButterBuds.
5. Add salt, sprinkling it over the top of the greens.
6. Cover and cook on High until boiling.
7. Reduce heat and cook about 30 minutes, or until greens are a dark green.
8. Turn them at least once during cooking to insure they all cook evenly.
9. Taste to determine when done.

Accompanies: Stove-Top Cornbread

Steamed Fresh Broccoli

This is my favorite way to prepare — and enjoy — broccoli. Notice I do not recommend a melted cheese sauce. If you insist on that, then add it. Personally, I like the broccoli by itself.

Ingredients:

1 steamer. You may use a retractable steamer in a large pot.
1 bunch of broccoli
Salt to taste
Butter, if desired, or ButterBuds

Preparation:

1. Place steamer in pot.
2. Add water until it is just below steamer.
3. Cut broccoli into smaller portions.
4. Put broccoli into steamer.
5. Sprinkle ButterBuds on top if you decide to use this.
6. Cover, bring to a boil.
7. Reduce heat to Medium.
8. Cook about 20 to 25 minutes.
9. Serve with melted butter, if desired.

Fresh Vegetable Sauté

"Yellow squash and zucchini squash combined with carrots cut in bite-size diagonal pieces make a particularly attractive vegetable dish. Snow peas and diagonally cut pieces of asparagus are also most attractive. The point is that any combination of vegetables, slightly seasoned and buttered, makes a delicious accompaniment to any meal! Vegetables can be parboiled, refreshed, and held all day if necessary." Betty Davis wrote that. I take her word for it.

Preparation:

1. Cut into bite-size pieces any of the following fresh vegetables: broccoli, yellow squash, zucchini squash, snow peas, asparagus, carrots.
2. Parboil in boiling salted water until crisp-tender.
3. Refresh in ice water to retain color and retard cooking process.
4. Drain and hold until ready to serve.
5. Before serving, heat 4 tablespoons butter and 2 tablespoons cooking oil in a skillet.
6. Add any combination of the above vegetables.
7. Toss quickly while shaking the pan.
8. Add salt and freshly ground pepper to taste.
9. Serve immediately.

Asparagus Casserole

Asparagus grows on you; that is, you have to teach yourself to like it. Raw, it tastes like peanuts; cooked, it tastes like asparagus. All the mushrooms — how did the mushrooms and beans work, by the way? — and other stuff make this dish a delight.

Ingredients:

2 cans asparagus tips
1 can cream of cheddar soup
1 or 2 boiled eggs
1 can cream of mushroom soup
1/4 teaspoon pepper, or more if you like it
1 cup buttered bread crumbs

Preparation:

1. Boil eggs, and while they cook,
2. Mix: cream of cheddar soup, cream of mushroom soup.
3. Place asparagus in a casserole dish.
4. Pour soup mixture over asparagus.
5. Sprinkle pepper over top.
6. Sprinkle bread crumbs over top.
7. Bake at 350 degrees for 25 minutes, or until bubbly.
8. As casserole bakes, peel and slice eggs.
9. Remove casserole from oven, arrange sliced eggs on top, and serve.

Creamed Celery Almandine

I can't remember where this recipe came from, so I don't know who to blame...or credit. In the old days I enjoyed all that cream and butter, and now I leave that to you.

Ingredients:

2 cups celery chopped
2 tablespoons butter or margarine
1/4 cup whipping cream
1 tablespoon flour, presifted
1/8 cup chicken broth
1 tablespoon chopped chives
1/4 cup toasted almonds

Preparation:

1. Melt butter.
2. Add celery and sauté.
3. Cover and cook for 2 minutes at medium heat.
4. Add whipping cream and stir.
5. Heat 1 minute uncovered.
6. Add flour and blend in.
7. Add chicken broth.
8. Cover and cook 1 minute.
9. Add chives.
10. Add almonds.
11. Cover and cook until creamy.

Green Chili Casserole

This casserole dish is particularly good as an accompaniment to beef dishes. It is simple to prepare, and it holds well in a warmer. It is another of Betty Davis' contributions to this book.

Ingredients:

3 4-ounce cans green chilis
1 cup cheddar cheese, grated
4 eggs
1/2 teaspoon salt
1/2 teaspoon dry mustard
1/2 cup whole milk or cream

Preparation:

1. Preheat oven to 350 degrees.
2. Split chilis and remove seeds, drain.
3. Beat together: eggs, salt, dry mustard, milk.
4. Grease a 9-inch square pyrex baking dish.
5. Layer chilis and cheese until gone.
6. Pour egg mixture over chilis and cheese.
7. Bake for 30 minutes.

Cheese Grits

Here comes my Southern-ness again. A Yankee fellow, eating breakfast in the South for the fourth consecutive morning, and staring at grits each time, asked a cafe waitress why they were served even when not ordered. "It's the law here," she told him. Well, that may not be a law, but it oughta be. Grits is good! This dish is not a breakfast item, however, unless you are desperate for grits. I would serve this one for dinner, if I could still eat cheese.

Ingredients:

3/4 cup grits
3 cups water
1/2 pound sharp cheddar cheese, grated
2 teaspoons seasoned salt
3/4 stick butter or margarine
Tabasco sauce, dash

Preparation:

1. Cook grits in boiling water about 20 minutes, or until they have absorbed nearly all the water and are near the consistency of mashed potatoes.
2. Add: cheese, salt, butter or margarine, Tabasco sauce.
3. Stir.
4. Place in baking dish.
5. Cover and bake at 250 degrees for 1 hour.

3

Salads

T ime was, I didn't care much for salads. Then came my experience with marriage. Even in the days before I was Liberated, my spouse liked salads. Any kind of salads. Most women eat them for lunch — I mean that is about all they eat — and even dinner, in the belief that salads will make them look like Cher in the hips and Dolly elsewhere. I don't think any amount of any kind of salad could accomplish that miracle, but it is a nice thought.

Anyway, my spouse does like salads, and I have grown to appreciate them as well. I expect my favorite is potato salad, followed by green salad, and then fruit salad. I can even find a blessing in tuna salad and chicken salad. Now all these salads have different functions. Those with meat in them are intended to *be* a meal, while the others are supposed to complement a meal in which you find the meat elsewhere provided. I don't care if you defy these rules and work it vice versa, and I don't think Ms. Manners will be offended either.

What most of us prepare for our own table is the tossed green salad. It is filling without being fattening, unless you load it with gooey dressings filled with fat. Without the dressing, I expect that a salad requires about as much calorie-burning exercise to eat as the amount of calories you consume. But who can stand much of that?

Mostly, lettuce is intended to be a part of some dish, not the whole thing. You have to have something to give flavor to lettuce, and most of the time I cheat and add some kind of dressing. A red wine vinegar is probably better for me, but with that I can still taste the lettuce. I usually use a small portion of Ranch or Thousand Island dressing in the low-calorie variety. The "low-calorie" label at least takes away some of the guilt.

You will never know how it feels to be sitting in a restaurant and hear Dr. Joe's voice saying from behind you, "Thousand Island dressing is NOT on your diet!" Since that humiliating experience, when we eat out I sit in a corner with my back to the wall, ready to throw my salad under the table. At home, I still use dressing. I guess what I am confessing is that I am a Closet Salad Eater.

All the salads in this section are easy to prepare, and will help fill out a meal. This is particularly useful when you are just learning the ropes as a HouseHusband and cook. It is difficult enough to get the meat dish and at least one vegetable prepared without having to worry about a salad. Obviously, some will be more appropriate with one kind of meal than another, but hey, you are intelligent, I don't have to say which. I will give you a hint: try the Mexican salad with one of the Mexican food recipes elsewhere. See how simple it is?

Cauliflower Salad

Cauliflower has to be useful for something, so you might as well use it this way. On top of the fact that it is healthful, it is another of those foods with Uppity Appeal. I can't use the cheese anymore, and without it you can taste the cauliflower. You might like it anyway.

Ingredients:

**1 head cauliflower
1 bell pepper, chopped
1/2 pound cheddar cheese, grated
6 to 8 stalks celery, sliced
1 bottle Caesar's creamy salad dressing
1 cup sour cream
3 tablespoons olive oil
Stuffed green olives**

Preparation:

1. Break cauliflower into bite-size pieces.
2. In a large bowl combine: cauliflower, bell pepper, cheddar cheese, celery, Caesar's creamy salad dressing, sour cream, olive oil, green olives.
3. Mix well.
4. Serve.

Chicken Salad

This is not necessarily a dish for those who are "chicken," (not a term synonymous with HouseHusbands at all), but for those who like chicken. It is an excellent selection if you cater an Uppity Woman's lunch for your UW and her friends in the UW Network.

Ingredients:

1 chicken
1/2 pound seedless grapes
1 can water chestnuts, chopped
1 package toasted almond slivers
1 cup celery, chopped
1 1/2 cups mayonnaise
1 1/2 teaspoons curry powder
1 1/2 teaspoons soy sauce

Preparation:

1. Cook chicken in boiling water until done, about 1 hour.
2. Allow to cool.
3. Remove bones and skin, chop meat into small pieces.
4. Combine: chicken, grapes, water chestnuts, almonds, celery, mayonnaise, curry powder, soy sauce.
5. Mix well.
6. Chill before serving.

Crab Salad

Crab salad will do nicely for the Uppity Woman's lunch. Crab meat is expensive, so everyone will be duly impressed with your extravagance and desire to make your Uppity Woman proud of you. Everyone likes crab, some because they think they should, some because they really like it, and some because it is ironic.

Ingredients:

1 can crab meat, drained
1/2 cup sour cream
2 teaspoons horseradish
1/4 teaspoon pepper
2 tablespoons Italian dressing

Preparation:

1. Mix together: crab meat, sour cream, horse-radish, pepper, Italian dressing.
2. Stir together well.
3. Serve with crackers.

This can be served as an hors d'oeuvre.

Fried Apples

Apples are good any way you eat them, even hot from the cooktop. Eating them can make you think of the wonderful places they grow, such as Washington State and Colorado. Anything that comes from mountain country is good.

Ingredients:

3 to 4 medium apples
3 tablespoons margarine
Cinnamon to taste

Preparation:

1. Cut apples in halves, remove core.
2. Cut into slices approximately 3/4-inch wide, then into small chunks.
3. Place in pot with enough water to cover bottom to prevent sticking or burning.
4. Place margarine on top.
5. Cover and cook at High heat until nearly boiling.
6. Reduce heat to Low, cook until apples are tender.
7. Place in serving dish and generously sprinkle cinnamon on top.

Fruit Salad

This recipe represents simplicity at its best, both in ease of prepa-
ration, nutrition, and taste. Leave out the sweetened cherries if
your Uppity Woman is dieting again.

Ingredients:

2 bananas, peeled
1 orange, peeled and chunked
1 apple, cored and chunked
1 can pineapple chunks
1/4 cup maraschino cherries
1/2 cup pecans, crumbled

Preparation:

1. Combine all ingredients.
2. Mix thoroughly.
3. Chill before serving.

Mexican Salad

This recipe is easily learned by observation. Upwardly Mobile Women (the stage just prior to becoming Uppity) who arrive home from meetings too near the deadline for having their potluck entry in the Church Supper Sweepstakes ready, at least to be artful and a contender in the evening's competition, make this salad because it is quick. Sometimes four or five UMWs in a small congregation will prepare it. If you have that many of the things to study (and little else from which to choose), you can make a careful inventory of the ingredients, estimate amounts of each, and create the thing yourself for the next supper — at home or at church.

Ingredients:

1 small bag of Fritos
1 head of lettuce
1 pound cheddar cheese, grated
1 onion, chopped
1 to 2 chopped tomatoes
1 to 2 cans pinto beans
3/4 bottle Catalina salad dressing

Preparation:

1. Mix all ingredients except Fritos.
2. Just before serving, add crushed Fritos.

Accompanies: Mexican Casserole, Mexican Corn Bread

Mystery Salad

What is the mystery? The mystery is why anyone would want to do this to an honorable commodity such as gelatin. Still, when you get all those things together, some women will eat it. One of my dear friends, Jewel Cates, put me on to this one.

Ingredients:

1 small package raspberry gelatin
1 pound can of stewed tomatoes, cut up
4 drops Tabasco sauce

Preparation:

1. Dissolve gelatin in 1/3 cup plus 2 tablespoons of boiling water.
2. Add: stewed tomatoes, Tabasco sauce.
3. Pour into lightly oiled gelatin mold.
4. Chill until set.
5. Serve with dressing made of :
   1 small carton sour cream
   1 teaspoon sugar
   salt to taste
   horseradish to taste

Chris' Potato Salad

My youngest son got his recipe out of some book, so here is a well-intentioned "thank you" to all writers of such material. Chris does well with this, so well that I always let him prepare it. That way he will have a head start on marriage.

Ingredients:

4 medium potatoes
1 tablespoon green parsley, chopped (or leaves)
1 teaspoon mustard
1/2 cup mayonnaise
1 small onion, diced
1 hard cooked egg, diced
1 teaspoon celery seed
1/3 of 2-ounce jar of pimento
Salt to taste

Preparation:

1. Boil potatoes until well done.
2. When they are cool enough, peel them.
3. Boil egg.
4. Dice: egg, potatoes.
5. Combine in a large bowl.
6. Add: onion, parsley, pimento, celery seed.
7. Salt to taste.
8. Mix in: mustard, mayonnaise.

Potato Salad

This is another way to make the same thing, not necessarily better, just a little different. I would leave out the yellow of the egg, but you may do as you wish in your own kitchen.

Ingredients:

5 to 6 potatoes cooked, peeled, and cubed
1 cup dill pickle, chopped
1/2 cup onion, chopped
2 eggs, hard cooked and chopped
1 cup bell pepper, chopped
1/4 teaspoon lemon pepper
1 teaspoon salt
1/2 cup mayonnaise
1/4 cup mustard
1 small jar pimento

Preparation:

1. Peel potatoes.
2. Boil them until a fork will penetrate them easily. Do not overcook or they will be "mushy."
3. Cut potatoes into bite-size pieces.
4. Add: dill pickle, onion, eggs, bell pepper, lemon pepper, salt, mayonnaise, mustard, pimento.
5. Stir thoroughly.
6. Chill before serving.

Sauerkraut Salad

Uppity Women come in all nationalities, so if you are married to a UW of German extraction, try this.

Ingredients:

**1 large can sauerkraut
1/2 cup bell pepper, chopped
1/2 cup celery, chopped
1/2 cup green onion, chopped
1 tablespoon pimentos
1/2 cup sugar
1/2 cup vinegar
1/4 cup salad oil**

Preparation:

1. Mix together: sauerkraut, bell pepper, celery, onion, pimento.
2. Heat the sugar, vinegar, and oil in a pot.
3. When sugar is dissolved, pour over the sauerkraut mixture.
4. Mix well.
5. Best if refrigerated overnight before serving.
6. This salad keeps well in the refrigerator.

Spinach Salad

Just as in the case of mushrooms, most women, Uppity and otherwise, like spinach. I don't think it is a Popeye obsession, but all of them, especially mothers, endorse the food value of spinach. You have to acquire a taste for spinach just as you do for asparagus. Persistence pays off. If you are not afraid you will punch some Bluto in the snout, eat plenty of it.

Ingredients:

1 bag fresh spinach
4 ounces blue cheese, crumbled
1 can french fried onion rings
1 can tomato soup
3/4 cup oil
3/4 cup vinegar
3/4 cup sugar
1/2 teaspoon salt
1 teaspoon dry mustard
1/4 teaspoon paprika
1 onion, quartered

Preparation:

1. Wash spinach and remove stems.
2. Tear leaves into small pieces.
3. In a bottle or other container mix: sugar, salt, dry mustard, paprika.
4. Add: tomato soup, oil, vinegar.
5. Mix well.
6. Drop in onion, but remove before serving.
7. Pour over spinach.
8. Top with blue cheese and onion rings.

4

Breads

Don't worry too much about making bread until you have mastered the more important skills of preparing meats, vegetables, and salads. Those things can a meal make. If you just *have* to have bread, remember what Leon Hale said about the "light bread people is ruinin' our women" by releasing them from this daily chore. What is good for the goose. . .Anyway, store-bought bread isn't all that good; you can do without it very well unless you eat leftovers in sandwiches.

When you are ready, try some of the following recipes for bread. Women who had the time — or took the time — to bake bread at home were at a premium in the days before Liberation. Now that they have more important things to do, such as painting their toe nails so they will not be embarrassed to wear open-toe high heels, women who bake bread have become an extinct species. It may be up to you to perpetuate the art of baking bread, pending the Revolution. After all, someone will have to show the women how to do it again. (Just kidding about the Revolution, honey.)

Hot Cross Bread

I wonder if this one came from Linda? Anyway, this is beyond the skill or patience of the novice HouseHusband. I am waiting to try it when I am more skilled.

Ingredients:

1 cup shortening
2/3 cup sugar
1 1/2 teaspoon salt
1 cup boiling water
2 eggs, beaten
1 package active dry yeast
1 cup lukewarm water
6 cups unsifted flour

Preparation:

1. Combine: shortening, sugar, salt.
2. Pour boiling water over this combination.
3. Stir until dissolved.
4. Add eggs.
5. Sprinkle the yeast into the lukewarm water and mix until dissolved.
6. Add to the above mixture.
7. Mix well.
8. Add flour and blend well.
9. Put in a covered bowl and refrigerate 4 hours at least.
10. About three hours before needed, knead dough for 2 to 3 minutes and shape into rolls or loaves.
11. Place into greased pans and let rise approximately 3 hours.
12. Bake at 400 degrees, 12 to 15 minutes for rolls,

or 17 to 20 minutes for loaves, until golden brown.
13. Butter top while still hot.

Dough will keep up to a week in refrigerator. Baked loaves can be frozen and warmed when ready to use.

Mexican Corn Bread

Remember Mexican Salad? Add this to the menu when you serve things Mexican. Be careful with the jalapeño.

Ingredients:

1 cup corn meal
2 eggs
1/2 teaspoon baking soda
1/4 cup bacon drippings, or suitable amount of
     margarine
1/2 pound cheese, grated
1 cup milk
1 small can cream-style corn
3/4 teaspoon salt
2 to 3 jalapeño peppers, chopped
1/2 cup onions, chopped

Preparation:

1. Combine all ingredients.
2. Mix well.
3. Place in greased cast-iron skillet.
4. Bake at 350 degrees for 45 minutes.
5. For muffins, bake at 425 degrees for 20 minutes.

Accompanies: Mexican Casserole, Mexican Salad

Stove Top Corn Bread

Aunt Jonnie taught my Uppity Woman how to make Stove Top Corn Bread, and then by and by she taught me. I wanted to learn. After all, if I had to make the greens and other things you just can't eat without corn bread if you are a Southerner, I surely did not want to leave this gap in my Liberation. You can do this a more complicated way in the oven, but this is quicker. Besides, there's real art in "flipping" the stuff in the skillet when one side is still in a liquid state. If you miss — splat!

Ingredients:

3/4 cup flour
3/4 cup white corn meal
1 teaspoon bacon drippings or margarine
1 teaspoon salt
1 teaspoon baking powder
1 egg, beaten
3/4 cup milk

Preparation:

1. Mix dry ingredients (flour, corn meal, baking powder, salt).
2. Add: milk, egg.
3. Mix to pasty consistency, adding a little more milk if necessary.
4. Heat drippings or margarine in small iron skillet until it shows heat (small bubbles will appear).
5. Reduce heat to Low and pour batter into skillet.
6. Cover.
7. Cook 10 minutes, covered.
8. Turn bread with metal spatula when bottom side is firm enough.

9. Cook 10 minutes longer, covered.
10. Remove by turning skillet upside down over plate.
11. Slice.
12. Serve with butter or margarine.

Accompanies: Anything, especially greens or stew. If you are really Southern, or smart, you will crumble leftover cornbread in a glass of milk. This is a special treat for a bed-time snack.

5

Desserts

Ordinarily I am not much on desserts, and I can't even blame Dr. Joe this time. It is not that I am sweet enough already — the only thing "sweet" in our house is the poodle — I just don't have much of a taste for sweet things. (No offense, honey.) One thing Uppity Women have in common, regardless of nationality or geography, is a sweet tooth. You have to be prepared to deal with this.

Here are a few recipes, mostly contributed by sympathetic friends, that you might try. I present them as they came to me without much endorsement because I have not prepared them myself. This may be a fatal confession in a book such as this, but I want to be honest with you.

Better Than Sex Cake

Jewel Cates' cake recipe has got to be the most mislabeled recipe in this whole book. If that doesn't communicate, I am not going to draw you any pictures in a family-oriented cookbook. Even so, what could be more appropriate to serve the overcommitted (in time) Uppity Woman?

Ingredients:

1 box yellow cake mix (without pudding)
1 box instant vanilla pudding
1/2 cup cooking oil
1/2 cup water
4 eggs
1 cup sour cream
1 bar German sweet chocolate, grated
1 6-ounce package butterscotch chips
1 6-ounce package chocolate chips
1 cup pecans

Preparation:

1. Beat together well: yellow cake mix, vanilla pudding mix, cooking oil, water, eggs, sour cream.
2. Add: grated German chocolate, 6-ounce package
   butterscotch chips, 6-ounce package chocolate
   chips, 1 cup pecans.
3. Mix well.
4. Well oil a bundt pan.
5. Pour in batter.
6. Bake in 350 degrees oven for 1 hour.

Buttermilk Chocolate Pudding Cake

Buttermilk is unusable any other way. You can't taste it once it is cooked, so if you have some, this is a good way to use it.

Ingredients:

2 cups sugar
1 cup cooking oil
2 eggs, beaten
2 cups flour
1 teaspoon vanilla
1/2 teaspoon salt
1 teaspoon soda
2 tablespoons cocoa
1/2 cup buttermilk
1 cup water

Preparation:

1. Combine: sugar, oil, eggs.
2. Beat well.
3. Combine dry ingredients: flour, salt, soda, cocoa.
4. Add to sugar mixture, stir well after each addition.
5. Blend in: buttermilk, water, vanilla.
6. Batter will be thin.
7. Pour into a 13 x 9 x 2 inch pan.
8. Bake at 350 degrees for 30 to 35 minutes.
9. Prepare icing by mixing together:
   1 box powdered sugar
   1 teaspoon vanilla
   2 tablespoons cocoa
   1/3 cup buttermilk
   1/4 cup melted margarine
10. Mix icing well and spread on hot cake.

Dump Cake

I find this another curious name. Do you suppose it came from a kitchen accident in the Early Days? This is contributed by Jewel Cates.

Ingredients:

1 8-ounce can crushed pineapple, drained
1 can cherry pie filling
1 yellow cake mix
1 cup chopped pecans
1 cup margarine, sliced

Preparation:

1. In a 9 x 13 x 2 inch baking pan, spread evenly on bottom: crushed pineapple, then cherry pie filling, then yellow cake mix, then chopped pecans.
2. Cover evenly with sliced margarine.
3. Bake in 325 degree oven for 1 hour.
4. Can be served with whipped cream or ice cream.

Martha's Peach Cobbler

Martha Emmons is one of my youngest friends. Martha started teaching high school students in the early 1920s, then moved on to the Baptist Vatican at Waco known as Baylor University. Whatever her age — and I won't ask — she has a twinkle in her eye that would dim a locomotive headlight, and a sense of adventure to match. Bless her, she wanted you to share her peach cobbler recipe.

Ingredients:

1/4 stick margarine
1 No. 2 can sliced peaches
3/4 cup milk
3/4 cup Bisquick
3/4 cup sugar

Preparation:

1. Melt butter in a Pyrex baking dish.
2. Pour in the sliced peaches.
3. Pour milk over peaches.
4. Mix together: Bisquick, sugar.
5. Pour over peaches.
6. Bake in a 350 degrees oven for 45 minutes, or until brown.

Mexican Cookies

My publisher, another Uppity Woman (I am surrounded by them), insisted that I add this recipe. She says it goes with all my Tex-Mex dishes.

Ingredients:

2 sticks butter or margarine
1 cup brown sugar
1 cup chopped pecans
Graham Crackers

Preparation:

1. Break apart enough Graham Crackers to cover the bottom of a jelly roll tray.
2. Combine margarine and sugar in a pot, bring to a boil and boil for 2 minutes.
3. Remove from heat and add chopped pecans.
4. Spread over the graham crackers.
5. Bake at 350 degrees for 8 minutes.
6. When cool break apart.

These are like Mexican pralines.

Mom's Sugar Cookies

Everybody's mom used to make sugar cookies. Where have all the mom's gone? To work! No more sugar cookies unless you bake them.

Ingredients:

1/2 cup shortening
1 cup sugar
2 eggs, well beaten
2 tablespoons milk
1 teaspoon vanilla
3 1/2 cups flour
2 teaspoons baking powder

Preparation:

1. Beat together: shortening, sugar.
2. Add: eggs, milk, vanilla.
3. Beat well.
4. Combine: flour, baking powder.
5. Gradually add flour and baking powder mixture to the shortening and sugar mixture.
6. This is difficult and hands may be used to work it into a good dough consistency.
7. Chill in refrigerator at least one hour before baking.
8. On floured surface, roll dough to desired thickness.
9. With cookie cutters, cut in desired shapes.
10. Bake on a lightly greased cookie sheet for 8 to 10 minutes at 375 degrees.

6

Breakfast Foods

Your mother told you that breakfast is the most important meal of the day. Television commercials, mostly for breakfast foods, confirm your mother's intuition. You know all the arguments that favor this claim. I will only add that nearly all the things normally eaten at breakfast taste good.

At our place, the day begins with coffee sipped while we let Jane Pauley, Bryant Gumble, and Willard Scott tell us the day's news, weather, and sports. Despite Liberation, my Uppity Woman usually fetches the coffee to the bedroom. When we have finished the coffee, learned the news, and reviewed the day's schedule, I go downstairs. An Uppity Woman's make-up preparation for a hard day of staff meetings, ribbon cuttings, and greetings to conventioneers requires more time than shaving and brushing of teeth. While she curls her hair and applies her make-up, I squeeze the fruit juice, toast the muffins, and do whatever else is done in the way of breakfast. *Her* share is then delivered back upstairs on a tray.

Wintertime, I will prepare something warm — except She doesn't like oatmeal. From this you may correctly deduce that She is not Scottish, as am I. In the old days this would have meant eggs and bacon for all in the house. Now we both opt for the lower calorie items mentioned above. Whatever your choice, if *you* have the responsibility for the kitchen, make sure everyone has some breakfast. The moms of the world have to be right.

Breakfast Meats

Bacon

Bacon is one of the most tasty meats available. It flavors anything well, and by itself is the perfect companion to eggs. I wish I could still have it on my plate.

Ingredients:

1 to 2 slices per person

Preparation:

1. Place bacon in frying pan.
2. Cook on High heat.
3. If you have a bacon press, use it — it will help keep bacon flat so it will cook evenly, and give the bacon a better appearance. Bacon tends to curl on the fatty ends and buckle in the middle. This is annoying when turning.
4. As bacon browns, turn it with fork or tongs so both sides will cook.
5. Repeat turning, if necessary.
6. When brown, but not black— this means you have overcooked it and probably smoked up the kitchen— remove and place on sheet of absorbent kitchen paper towels. Dab off excess grease with paper tower.
7. Save bacon drippings to season vegetables.

Ham

You don't have to be from Virginia or Kentucky to like ham, or work in the theatre to be one. When living on a farm in Missouri, I learned that ham gravy is the best of all gravies.

Ingredients:

1 to 2 slices per person

Preparation:

1. Place ham in a skillet.
2. Heat on High until ham is thoroughly warmed.
3. It is not necessary to brown ham as you do bacon and sausage — just make sure it is thoroughly cooked.
4. Precooked hams, the way they mostly are purchased in the supermarket, have been cooked and only require heating to degree desired.
5. Remove and place on absorbent paper towel.
6. Dab excess grease with paper towel.

Sausage

Most people automatically think of pork, but I have discovered turkey sausage! Apparently the taste mostly comes from the spices, because I can't tell any difference in the taste.

Ingredients:

1 to 2 links or patties per person

Preparation:

1. Place sausage in frying pan on stove.
2. Cook on High heat.
3. It may be necessary to add a little water to prevent sticking.
4. As bottom side browns, turn with fork, tongs, or spatula to brown other side.
5. Repeat until both sides are evenly browned.
6. Place on absorbent kitchen paper towel.
7. Dab grease from top side with paper towel.
8. Discard grease.

Cereals

Dry Cereal

Taste and prudence are your best guide. I prefer a natural cereal with as little sugar and salt added as possible. Shredded wheat, for example, just naturally tastes good.

Preparation:

1. Pour desired amount of cereal into a bowl.
2. Add sweetener, if desired, and milk. Try to eat before it gets too soggy.

Oatmeal

Three centuries ago Dr. Samuel Johnson's Dictionary identified "oats" as food for horses and Scotsmen. That must be why I like it. I am all Scot and have been called half a horse — the back half.

Ingredients:

1 1/2 cups water
1/4 teaspoon salt
2/3 cup oatmeal
Milk in desired amount (I use skim milk)
Sugar or other sweetener to taste

Preparation:

1. Put water into a pot.
2. Add salt.
3. Boil water.
4. Stir in oatmeal.
5. Cook 5 minutes, stirring occasionally.
6. Remove from heat, cover and let stand a few minutes before serving.
7. Add milk and sugar or other sweetener to taste.

Grits

Remember that it is the Law in the South that grits be a part of a breakfast served in a restaurant. At home, you may wait until dinner.

Ingredients:

2/3 cups grits
1 2/3 cups water
3/4 teaspoon salt

Preparation:

1. Add salt to water.
2. Boil water.
3. Add grits.
4. Reduce heat somewhat.
5. Boil 5 to 6 minutes, stirring frequently.
6. Remove from heat, serve hot.

Quick Cream of Wheat

Ingredients:

1 3/4 cups of water or milk
1/4 teaspoon salt
1/3 cup cream of wheat

Preparation:

1. Add salt to water or milk.
2. Bring to boil.
3. Slowly sprinkle in cream of wheat.
4. Stir constantly.
5. Return to boil.
6. Lower heat to Low.
7. Cook for 2 to 3 minutes or until thick.

Breakfast Breads

Toast

Any fool can make toast. Just stick one or two slices into the toaster or toaster-oven and let the machine do its thing. See Toaster, page 23.

English Muffin

Follow the directions given for making toast.

These handy devices can be used for nearly-homemade pizza. Slice in halves, spread pizza sauce and a slice of mozzarella cheese on top and bake until cheese is melted. But not in the morning! If you do eat this for breakfast, you may want to have a slice of "Better Than Sex" cake, too.

Biscuits

Basically, grocery stores make two varieties of biscuits available.
1. *Canned biscuits, and*
2. *Biscuits made with a mix.*

"Scratch" biscuits are not that different from Number 2, and are more complicated than most HouseHusbands of Uppity Women are willing to tackle.

Canned Biscuits

Lewis Grizzard calls these "whomp" biscuits. He derived the name from the necessity to "whomp" the can on the edge of the cabinet or a table to open it.

1. Preheat oven to 450 degrees.
2. Pull tab on package and remove.
3. Using edge of spoon, depress package on seam until can pops open, or "whomp" it on the edge of the cabinet.
4. Remove biscuits and arrange in circular pie pan, sides should be touching.
5. Place in oven until brown.

Biscuits From a Mix

Ingredients:

**2 cups Pioneer or Bisquick Mix
2/3 cup milk**

Preparation:

1. Preheat oven to 450 degrees.
2. Combine biscuit mix and milk, blending well.
3. Form dough into a ball.
4. Sprinkle a cutting board with more dry mix.
5. Turn dough 3 or 4 times on board.
6. Roll to 1/2-inch thickness.
7. Cut with a 2-inch cutter (or any clean, round-cupped object, such as a drinking glass).
8. Bake on lightly greased baking sheet until brown, about 10-12 minutes.

Eggs

Eggs are the basic of a cooked breakfast for many. If you can stand the cholesterol, nothing beats eggs for breakfast. Just the smell of them cooking quickens the appetite.

There are several easy ways to prepare them, including: fried or poached, scrambled, or in an omelet.

Fried-Poached

Ingredients:

1 to 2 eggs per person
1 tablespoon margarine
Water
Salt
Pepper

Preparation:

1. If you fried bacon or sausage in the same frying pan, pour the grease in a container to save for seasoning vegetables if you use it for this purpose.
2. Melt margarine over High heat until fully liquid and small bubbles appear.
3. Break eggs gently on edge of frying pan and place contents in pan.
4. As the clear liquid part of egg begins to turn white, add sufficient water (about 3 tablespoons) to prevent egg from sticking to pan.
5. Cover and reduce heat to Medium-High.
6. Cook about 2 to 3 minutes, or until white is firm.
7. You may cook longer if you wish the yolk firm, or

turn over with a spatula for over-easy style eggs.
8. Lift eggs with spatula and place on plate.
9. Season with salt and black pepper to taste.
10. If toast is desired, begin the toast when you cover eggs. The toast and eggs will be done at about the same time.
11. Serve with bacon or sausage if desired.

Scrambled

Even non-HouseHusbands often enjoy scrambling eggs.

Ingredients:

1 to 2 eggs per person
Salt
Pepper
1/3 cup milk or water
Margarine

Preparation:

1. Break all eggs into a bowl, being careful that no shell fragments get in with the eggs.
2. Add: salt and pepper to taste.
3. Add 1/3 cup milk — more will be needed if scrambling more than 3 to 4 eggs.
4. Beat until thoroughly mixed.
5. Heat frying pan over High heat until hot.
6. Pour contents into frying pan.
7. Stir constantly with wooden or plastic spoon.
8. As eggs begin to thicken, be sure to keep them from sticking. Reduce heat if necessary.
9. As eggs near done, add 1 to 2 tablespoons of margarine and stir until margarine is melted.
10. Serve with toast or bacon or sausage.

Sausage and Egg Casserole

My days of eating all those eggs and sausages are over, but I still make dishes I can't consume. If you can have all this, you enjoy it!

Ingredients:

8 slices fresh white bread, cubed
1 pound ground pork sausage
2 cups American cheese, grated
4 to 6 eggs
3/4 teaspoon dry mustard
2 1/2 cups milk
1 can cream of mushroom soup
1/2 cup milk

Preparation:

1. Grease a 9 x 13 x 2 inch baking pan.
2. Place cubed bread in the bottom.
3. Brown and drain the pork sausage.
4. Spread sausage over the bread cubes.
5. Sprinkle with the grated cheese.
6. In a small bowl, mix together: eggs, dry mustard, milk.
7. Pour over the sausage and bread cubes.
8. Refrigerate overnight.
9. When ready to bake, mix together: cream of mushroom soup, 1/2 cup milk.
10. Pour over top of casserole.
11. Bake at 300 degrees for 1 1/2 hours.
12. Serves 8 to 10.

Bacon can be substituted for sausage.

Omelets

Onion Potato Omelet

There are several ways to prepare omelets. Here is a good one.

Ingredients:

8 eggs, beaten
2 large potatoes, diced
1 bell pepper, diced
1 onion, diced
3 tablespoons butter or margarine

Preparation:

1. In an electric skillet, melt butter *or* margarine.
2. Add: potatoes, bell pepper, onion.
3. Stir.
4. Cover and cook on Medium-High heat until tender.
5. Add beaten eggs.
6. Stir well.
7. Cover and cook until eggs set.
8. Cut into squares and serve.

Judy's Omelet

Guess who used to prepare this one? My Uppity Woman, of course. She likes it for a Sunday evening snack.

Ingredients:

2 eggs
2 tablespoons onion, chopped
1 tablespoon bell pepper, chopped
2 tablespoons butter
Salt and pepper to taste
1/4 cup cheddar cheese, grated

Preparation:

1. Beat eggs.
2. Add: salt and pepper.
3. Melt one tablespoon of butter into a 10-inch frying pan.
4. Sauté: onion, bell pepper until onions are clear.
5. Melt second tablespoon of butter.
6. Pour eggs into hot frying pan. Do not stir.
7. As eggs dry, on one side of eggs, add: onion, bell pepper, cheese.
8. Fold egg in half with spatula.
9. Serve.

Fresh Fruit

Grapefruit

Ingredients:

1 grapefruit per person or two persons

Preparation:

1. Slice grapefruit in half. Most persons will eat only half a grapefruit, so if no one is there to share (often Uppity Women have early breakfast meetings), save remaining half by covering in plastic wrap. Refrigerate.
2. With a grapefruit slicing knife, cut the meat of the fruit down to the peeling along the convenient division lines provided by nature.
3. With the same knife, insert the curved end of the blade between the meat and the peel and gently slice in a circle, following the contour of the peel until each slice is forced from the peel.
4. Serve in a small bowl with sweetener, if desired.

Orange Slices

Preparation:

1. Peel orange.
2. Slice orange, cross-cutting through natural divisions.
3. Remove seeds.
   or
1. Do not peel orange.
2. Slice, cross-cutting the natural divisions.
3. On a cutting board cut each slice in half.

Cantaloupe

When available, nothing beats a chilled cantaloupe for breakfast.

Preparation:

1. Place in refrigerator at least 12 hours before breakfast.
2. Slice in half along natural lines of the peel.
3. Scrape seeds from center.
4. Eat with spoon, being careful to stop before you get all the way to peel.

Spreads

Butter

Naturally butter tastes best, but has butterfat. That is what makes it taste good.

Margarine

Margarine is a little cheaper and, if you need to avoid fats, it may be better for you. Try a corn oil margarine which does not have cholesterol.

Preserves

My favorite is fig preserves, followed by blackberry, strawberry, and grape. Goes well on any breakfast bread.

Beverages Other Than Fruit Juice

Ice Water

The best there is. Especially good with eggs.

Milk

Nutritious and good for drinking from a glass as well as eating with cereal.

Beer

Only if you think you are Kris Kristofferson and you want to sing "Sunday Morning Coming Down."

Juices

The most common juices connected with breakfast
are:
    Grapefruit
    Orange
    Tomato
    V-8

*All juices are tastier if fresh. If possible, obtain an electric juicer —
the hand operated kind are less efficient and a lot more work.
Then pray for mild weather in Florida, Southern California, and
the Rio Grande Valley.*

Preparation:

1. Cut oranges or grapefruit in half.
2. Plug in juicer.
3. Place glass under spout of juicer.
4. Apply half of fruit to juicer. This engages juicer.
5. Push down and squeeze slightly to insure complete efficiency.
6. Combining orange and grapefruit juices produces a taste different from each that is good for a change, and gives you the grapefruit without the heavy or sour taste of the fruit, if you do not care for it straight.

You must use canned tomato and V-8 juice.

If you don't have a juicer for orange or grapefruit,
canned concentrates are a convenient if less tasty
substitute. Follow instructions on can. Some suggest
a 3 to 1 ratio for adding water, others suggest a 4 to 1
ratio.

Serving Breakfast

An ideal breakfast to serve your Uppity Woman consists of the following:

1. 1 fried-poached egg
2. 1/2 slice English muffin
3. Salt and pepper in silver or cut-glass matching shakers.
4. 1 cup coffee, with cream and sugar if desired.
5. 1 red or yellow rose in a crystal vase.
6. 1 linen napkin.
7. 1 fork, knife, spoon (each).
8. Arrange on a bed tray and serve at the assigned hour.

This will require the HouseHusband to rise at least 30 minutes prior to serving the Uppity Woman.

Of course, if you don't have time for all this because she must leave for an early meeting, the juice and muffin served as she curls her hair will have to do.

7

Lunch

Lunch, that marvelous break in the workday so utilized by American business titans as another opportunity to make deals, should be something more. It should be experienced as intended originally, a chance to interrupt the workday and enjoy a leisurely meal with a good friend, or even your Uppity Woman, if she is free.

Lunch has been exploited for years. Michael Korda, well-known author on the subject of power in the corporate community, claims that a good portion of the business morning is spent in selecting suitable luncheon partners and that the lunch table in chic restaurants has replaced the office desk as the altar of commerce.

Now they have even invaded breakfast. When the two-martini lunch came under closer scrutiny by the Internal Revenue Service (does it really take two martinis to close a deal?), breakfast became the perfect alternative. The two-fried egg breakfast at, shudder, 6:45 or 7 a.m. is the latest degradation of western society. Your Uppity Woman may not be able to escape this loss of civilization, but perhaps you can.

If you do not go home to lunch, you should consult a good restaurant guide appropriate for your area. Seek out the least expensive places where good food at reasonable prices is still a mark of pride. If there aren't any of these left in your area, you may take your lunch to work with you. Avoid this unless you are assured of pleasing company and are free from the pressures of work. Getting the company is up to you. I would recommend taking leftovers to warm up if your work place has a microwave available, because your own cooking at the right temperature is the best thing you can have. If a microwave is unavailable, try a thermos filled with hot soup. If carrying a thermos is not practical, bring a sandwich and some fruit. If that is not possible, you may as well just go back to work.

Assuming that occasionally you will need to prepare something for lunch on a nonworking day, or when you are supposed to be home with the flu, here are a few suggestions in the soup-salad-sandwich line.

Soups

There are a number of good tasting commercial soups available in cans or in instant mixes. If interested in this kind of quick fix, select the one you want and follow the instructions on the label. The novice HouseHusband can do this easily. Usually these soups are no more complicated than turning on the burner, employing the can into a saucepan, stirring in a little water (or not, depending upon the instructions), and waiting for the bubbles, your tip-off that the soup is ready.

If you desire something a little more interesting, try one of the following recipes.

Chicken and Ham Soup

This is a good noonday meal. Warm, nutritious, and reasonably fast.

Ingredients:

2 slices bacon
1 cup ham, cut into cubes
2 tablespoons onion, chopped
1/4 teaspoon thyme leaves, crushed
1 can cream of chicken soup
1 can chicken noodle soup
Milk
2 hard cooked eggs, diced
1 cup cut green beans

Preparation:

1. In large pan, cook bacon until crisp.
2. Remove bacon and crumble.

3. Brown ham.
4. Add: onion, thyme.
5. Sauté until onion is tender.
6. Add, stirring in: cream of chicken soup, chicken noodle soup, milk sufficient to fill one of the now empty soup cans, eggs, beans.
7. Heat, stirring occasionally, until all ingredients are hot.
8. Garnish top with crumbled bacon.

Elephant Soup

For the HouseHusband or Uppity Woman who goes on safari.

Ingredients:

1 elephant
1/2 bushel pepper
1 bushel salt
100 cloves garlic
3 rabbits

Preparation:

1. Kill elephant.
2. Skin and cut into bite-size pieces.
3. Cover with water.
4. Boil for 40 hours.
5. Add: salt, pepper, garlic.
6. Add rabbits if your Uppity Woman doesn't mind hare in her soup.
7. Serve hot.

Unless your Uppity Woman is a Republican, you will never need to make this dish.

(I am kidding, of course. Even HouseHusbands have a little humor.)

Garden Vegetable Soup

This is a super soup to prepare if you have a garden. For one thing, it is a way to utilize all those things you grow.

Ingredients:

2 cups fresh tomatoes chopped, or
2 cans tomatoes
1 16-ounce can tomato sauce
2 cups water
1 onion, chopped
1 cup celery, sliced
1 cup carrots, sliced
1 cup fresh green beans
1 cup yellow crookneck squash
1 cup zucchini squash
1 teaspoon salt, or to taste
Sweet basil and thyme, a pinch
2 teaspoons chili powder

Preparation:

1. Combine: tomatoes, tomato sauce, water, salt, pinch of sweet basil and thyme, chili powder.
2. Bring to boil and then reduce to simmer.
3. Add: onion, celery, carrots.
4. Simmer about 15 minutes.
5. Add: green beans, squash.
6. Simmer until all vegetables are tender.
7. Delicious with hot French bread.
8. For a beefy flavor, you can add 1 package of Lipton's Beefy Onion Soup Mix and omit the salt.

Gazpacho

HouseHusbands probably will not like this stuff, but I have never seen a woman, Uppity or otherwise, who could turn it down.

Ingredients:

1 clove garlic, chopped
3 pounds tomatoes, chopped
2 cucumbers, sliced thin
1/2 cup bell pepper, minced
1/2 cup onion, minced
2 cups iced tomato juice
1/3 cup olive oil
3 tablespoons vinegar
Salt to taste
Pepper to taste
1/4 teaspoon Tabasco sauce

Preparation:

1. Chop garlic to smallest possible pieces.
2. Peel and chop tomatoes.
3. Combine.
4. Peel and slice cucumbers and add them.
5. Add: peppers, onions, tomato juice, olive oil, vinegar, salt and pepper, Tabasco.
6. Cover and chill.
7. Serve in chilled bowl.

Gazpacho Gringo

Women adore this soup, too. Soup was not intended by nature to be eaten cold, except maybe by the French or the Italians. You can put ice in this soup and drink it from a glass, if you choose.

Ingredients:

4 to 5 ripe tomatoes, peeled
2 medium cucumbers, peeled
3 medium squash, peeled
1 bell pepper, seeded and deribbed
1/2 onion
1 clove garlic
2 tablespoons vinegar
1 tablespoon olive oil
1 teaspoon hot sauce or Tabasco, or to taste
Salt and pepper to taste

Preparation:

1. Place all ingredients into a blender.
2. Add water to the top.
3. Puree.
4. You may omit any of the vegetable ingredients except the tomato.

Quick Chicken Soup

Here is a quick recipe using all commercial ingredients. Even the novice HouseHusband can do this.

Ingredients:

1 can cream of chicken soup
1 can cream of mushroom soup
1 can cream of celery soup
1 5-ounce can chunk chicken
3 cans milk
1 small roll jalapeño cheese

Preparation:

1. Pour chicken, mushroom, and celery soups into pot.
2. Add: 3 cans of milk, jalapeño cheese.
3. Bring to a boil.
4. Add chunk chicken.
5. Simmer for 5 minutes.

Onion Wine Soup

Omit the wine and make onion soup if the alcohol offends you.

Ingredients:

5 large onions, chopped
5 cups beef broth
1/4 cup butter
1/2 cup celery leaves
1 large potato, sliced
1 cup dry white wine
1 tablespoon vinegar
1 tablespoon sugar
1 cup light cream
1 tablespoon parsley
Salt to taste
Pepper to taste

Preparation:

1. Melt butter in large saucepan.
2. Sauté onions in butter until well coated.
3. Add: beef broth, celery leaves, potato slices.
4. Heat until mixture boils.
5. Cover and simmer 30 minutes.
6. Pour mixture in blender, blend.
7. Pour back into saucepan and add: wine, vinegar, sugar.
8. Simmer for five minutes.
9. Stir in: cream, parsley, salt, pepper.
10. Heat thoroughly but remove before soup boils.

Potato Soup

You don't have to be Polish or German to like potato soup.

Ingredients:

6 medium potatoes, diced
2 medium onions, chopped
1/2 cup celery, chopped
2 quarts water
1/2 teaspoon coarse black pepper
1/2 teaspoon salt
2 tablespoons flour
2 tablespoons butter
1 cup cream
1/2 cup parsley
1/2 teaspoon dill seed, ground

Preparation:

1. Peel potatoes and dice them.
2. Boil potatoes with onions and celery in 2 quarts water until tender.
3. Remove vegetables but save water.
4. Blend vegetables in blender.
5. Return blended vegetables to saved water.
6. Mix together: salt, flour, cream.
7. Stir mixture into vegetable blend.
8. Add: parsley, dill.
9. Heat to desired temperature and serve.

Sausage Soup

This takes awhile, but if you have the time it might be worth it.

Ingredients:

1 pound link sausage
1 onion, chopped
1 can black-eyed peas or pinto beans
2 cans tomatoes
1 can whole kernel corn
1/4 teaspoon garlic salt
1 teaspoon salt
1/2 teaspoon pepper

Preparation:

1. Cut sausage into 1-inch lengths.
2. Place sausage in a soup pot and add: onion, black-eyed peas, tomatoes, corn, garlic salt, salt, pepper.
3. Cook covered for 35 minutes.
4. Add water if company comes in.

Luncheon (or Dinner) Salad

*Salads offer the opportunity to be truly creative. You can put
almost anything edible in the darn things, and as long as you do
not get too much of any one ingredient in it you can still brag
about the results. HouseHusbands do not have to be especially
diverse in this area, so we will settle for a basic tossed salad. You
may consult the SALAD section for additional ideas.*

Tossed Salad

Ingredients:

**1/2 to 3/4 head of lettuce, cut into small pieces
1 tomato, cut into small pieces
1/2 cucumber, sliced
2 to 3 green onions chopped, including tops
1/2 bell pepper
1 carrot, sliced thinly
1/4 cup cheddar cheese, grated
1/4 cup olives**

Preparation:

1. Wash all ingredients.
2. You may want to peel cucumber and carrot before slicing.
3. Combine all ingredients.

You may want to top with bacon bits or croutons.

Sandwiches

*The sandwich is allegedly named for a famous nobleman, the
Earl of Sandwich. The Earl ordered food placed between slices of
bread brought to his gambling table so he would not have to take
time away from a more important endeavor to do something as
unsporting as eating. Like computers and telephones, his inven-
tion was a mixed blessing. Likely, this is the kind of food your
Uppity Woman started serving when more worthy claims on her
time began to surface. Still, there is nothing wrong with a good
sandwich, especially for lunch.*

*Here are a few examples, easily made, that will help you survive
until dinner when more daring recipes await you.*

Bologna (or Any Luncheon Meat) Sandwich

*Varieties of luncheon loaf made with turkey meat are available.
The spices added to turkey make it taste like bologna, pastrami,
ham, or other varieties. You can't tell the difference, and you do
consume less fat.*

Ingredients:

**2 slices of bread, toasted if you prefer
1 to 2 slices of bologna
1 slice cheese (optional)
1 leaf lettuce
1 to 2 slices of tomato**

Preparation:

1. Toast bread.
2. With a knife, spread mayonnaise or salad dressing on both pieces of bread.
3. On the "spread" side of one slice, layer the following: bologna, cheese, lettuce, tomatoes.
4. Lay other "spread" slice on top.

Bacon and Tomato Sandwich

Try this for breakfast. It contains cereals, protein, and a fresh vegetable, which pleases dietitians. It makes a good lunch, and dinner too. My friend Max Lale, who couldn't resist putting a little humor on his recipe card, contributed this version.

1. Catch a true vine-ripened East Texas tomato, preferably from a roadside stand in Harrison County.
2. Peel, slice gently, and set aside until bacon is done. (You may drink the remaining juice out of the plate later.)
3. Fry bacon in its own grease in an iron skillet. A microwave won't do. If you have a cholesterol problem, you may blot the excess fat with a paper towel.
4. Depending on the number of tomatoes you have sliced and the number of bacon strips you have fried, lightly brown a number of bread slices in the oven on both sides. Use home-baked bread, if you are lucky. Again, no microwave.
5. Combine the tomato slices, bacon, and the bread. Be generous with the tomatoes and bacon.
6. Salt and pepper to taste.
7. Slather with mayonnaise.
8. Eat quickly while the oven heat is still palpable.

B L T

This sandwich is known everywhere. Why not in your own kitchen?

Ingredients:

2 slices of bread, toasted
4 to 6 slices of bacon
3 slices of tomato
2 leaves of lettuce
Mayonnaise or another salad dressing

Preparation:

1. Fry bacon.
2. Save grease for flavoring vegetables.
3. Drain bacon on paper towel.
4. Toast bread.
5. Spread mayonnaise *or* salad dressing on *one* side of each slice of bread.
6. On one slice of the "spread" side, layer: bacon, lettuce, tomatoes.
7. Lay "spread" side of other slice of bread on top.
8. Slice into four triangular pieces.

Peanut Butter and Jelly Sandwich

You don't have to be Dennis the Menace to like this old standard.

Ingredients:

1 jar peanut butter
1 jar jelly (your choice)
2 slices bread

Preparation:

1. On one slice of bread, spread peanut butter as thick as you want.
2. Spread jelly on the other slice of bread.
3. Place them together, spread sides in.

I have heard of weird people from Mississippi who spread on a layer of mayonnaise, too, but I have never actually seen this done.

Picnic Pimento Cheese

Easy to make ahead of time and an old picnic standard.

Ingredients:

**1 pound American cheese (half American and half cheddar will give it extra class), grated
1 large jar pimentos, diced
Salad dressing to create desired consistency
1 onion, finely chopped
Salt and pepper to taste
Garlic powder, dash**

Preparation:

1. Grate the cheese into a large bowl.
2. Stir in pimentos.
3. Blend in the salad dressing.
4. Add: onion, salt, pepper, garlic powder.
5. Place in the refrigerator.
6. Ready to spread any time, but flavors reinforce each other by the second day.

Side Edibles

You may want to munch along on something to accompany your sandwich.

Try:
Potato chips
Fritos
Tortilla chips
Wheat Thins
Cheez-its
Any other little thing in a box or bag.

Beverages

Beverages for the luncheon vary depending on tastes, times, and the activities of the afternoon. Do not try *three* martinis if the afternoon is going to find you involved in contract negotiations or interpersonal relations more complicated than helping someone sharpen a pencil.

As with breakfast, there is nothing wrong with water. Everyone needs more of the stuff than they usually take time to drink, and it will not leave a telltale odor on your breath as will beer and wine. *One* beer or *one* glass of wine is all right, but only if you are having Mexican, German, Polish, Italian, or some other ethnic food the drink will complement. Do not exceed this level or the boss will be the first to know. This is the case unless you have invited *Her* to lunch and She is a true Uppity Woman. In that case you must match Her drink for drink regardless of the consequences. After all, you are not *Her* HouseHusband, and someone has to take up for the rest of us.

Assuming that water is not what you want, try iced or hot tea, coffee, milk, or fruit juice. All are better for you, they generally taste better at that hour of the day, and you can return to work with only your belly full.

8

Dinner

Dinner (Supper)

Now we come to the most challenging and, at the same time, most rewarding time of the day for the HouseHusband. Your full potential as Lord of the Kitchen can be realized in assembling repasts that will surprise and please your Uppity Woman as well as yourself.

It begins when you walk through the door at 5:15 p.m. Your youngest will immediately ask, "When's supper?" You note that he is at this point uninterested in *what* you will prepare. His consuming interest is how soon it will be ready. Do not let this bother you. Whatever you fix will be of little consequence. It will either disappear into his gut in large, unchewable blobs or else he will pick out the olives from the salad and the mushrooms from the sauce and will shun your delicate casserole and exotic vegetable dishes altogether. So, the best answer is, "About an hour and a half." This will give you plenty of time to consult *Helpful Cooking Hints for HouseHusbands of Uppity Women*, assemble the cooking utensils and various ingredients, and have the meal prepared in time for the Arrival of the Uppity Woman.

You usually can count on The Arrival, with fanfare, just as you take the roast from the oven or lift the corn from the boiling water. Be nice. She has had a hard day. You can tell this from little signs. Her brief case will flop on the nearest chair, her high-heeled shoes miraculously will disengage themselves from her feet on the second and third steps into the room, and, if it is winter, her coat will sail toward the couch. Lines of care earned defending the community from dragons will crease her countenance. Through it all she will manage a smile of hello, and perhaps, if you are not still holding the steaming corn in front of you, she will give you an affectionate kiss.

If she is a drinking woman, that is, a woman who takes a cocktail or a glass of white wine either before or with the meal, it is a good idea to have it ready. If she is a teetotaler, this step should be omitted.

Seat her at the table you have prepared for her. If the breakfast rose is not wilted, it should be in the middle of the table. Otherwise, the table is dominated by the meat dish. Whether it is red meat, fish, or fowl determines everything else.

The meat dish is the basis of the meal unless, of course, you are both vegetarians. Now there is not one thing wrong with an all-vegetable, or a vegetable-and-fruit, or an all-fruit meal. On occasion. Since you do the cooking, and you like meat, well then you can have it if you want it. If you prepared roast, steak, or some other red meat, select two (or three) of the following vegetables to accompany it.

Sidney's Potatoes
Okra and Tomatoes
Country Style Yellow Squash
Fresh Green Beans

You may want to include a Tossed Salad and, if it is one of THOSE days, "Better than Sex" cake.

If you have prepared fish, try two of these.

Scalloped Potatoes
Steamed Broccoli
Stuffed Baked Potatoes
Squash Croquettes
Tossed Salad

If you prepared fowl (chicken, turkey) try some of these.

Buttered Rice
Asparagus Casserole
Steamed Squash
Garden Fresh Greens or Beans
New Potatoes
Stove Top Corn Bread (if you selected the greens)

Bread

We have already agreed with Leon Hale's friend that the "light bread people" have ruined our women, so unless it is absolutely necessary, do not serve the kind of bread that you buy in stores that is already sliced. With stew or most vegetables, corn bread is great. Rolls that you heat in the oven are acceptable. And French bread, sliced at one- to two-inch intervals not-quite-all-the-way through with garlic spread and/or butter between the slices, is excellent with any spaghetti dish.

Soups and Salads

For a discussion on the philosophy and preparation of salads see **Salads**, page 153 and **Lunch**, page 220. Anything appropriate there will fit here just as well. Soups should be light and not too filling, and served in smaller portions.

Beverages

What's wrong with water? It is still the best bet. However, it is simply not dinner at our house without iced tea. This is as true on January 4 as it is on July 4. Hot tea is for Yankees and the English anyway, but if you insist, you may have it. As with lunch, beer is fine if the food is appropriate (Mexican, Italian, German, Polish).

A good wine with dinner is appropriate for those who like it. Remember: red wine with red meat, white wine with fish or fowl, and rosé wine if you are indecisive. Remember, too: this is your kitchen, so if you want white wine with a steak, what the heck, go for it!

Coffee is great after a meal, unless you are an insomniac. If so, try decaffeinated coffee *and* tea.

Need an After-Dinner Snack?

These are best avoided, and will always be regretted the next morning when stepping on the bathroom scales. Do not encourage an Uppity Woman to indulge in snacks unless you leave early for work and can escape her wrath for her being twelve ounces over the previous day's reading. As the cook, this is automatically your fault.

If you cannot avoid preparing her an After-Dinner Snack, try popcorn made in an air popper. This method avoids the cooking oil required by other methods (which is full of calories) and provides a lighter popped corn. Likely, she will get you to melt butter to pour over it, negating the advantage gained by the air method, but try to dissuade her if you can. When you lose, use a low calorie, cholesterol-free margarine, if possible. This will taste about the same but will be better for you. After you have made it for her, how can you resist having some too?

9

Sample Menus

$\mathbf{A}$ wide variety of foods that may be combined in various ways await your selection. Of course, the choice of the daily menu is up to you. You will wish to take into account such things as the Uppity Woman's general likes and dislikes, her food allergies, and her weight. There is no need to prepare a meal that will make her turn up her nose, break out in a rash, or gain unwanted pounds. But the decision of what to serve is up to you because *you* are going to cook the meals.

Several factors will flavor your decision:

1. What do *you* want to eat?
2. Do *you* have the time after work and before her evening commitments to get the meal done?
3. Do *you* have all the necessary ingredients?
4. Have *you* the ability to cook it?

When *you* have achieved an acceptable alignment of at least three of the questions, press on!

There are many things you can prepare that are not in this book, but the following suggestions include dishes that are covered here.

Monday

Breakfast:
Orange or grapefruit juice
English muffin with
    butter
Coffee
Glass of water

Lunch:
B L T Sandwich
Potato chips
Vegetable Soup
Tea or Coffee

Dinner:
Chicken Delight
Steamed Broccoli
Sidney's Potatoes
Fruit Salad
Tea and/or Coffee

Tuesday

Breakfast:
Fruit juice
Dry Cereal
Toast
Coffee

Lunch:
Leftover Chicken Delight,
    or
Sandwich of your choice,
    or
Chicken and Ham Soup
Tea or Coffee

Dinner:
Pepper Steak
Stuffed Baked Potatoes
Fresh Greens
Tossed Salad
Tea and/or Coffee

Wednesday

Breakfast:
Fruit slices
Oatmeal
Toast

Lunch:
Leftover Pepper Steak, or
Chicken and Ham Soup
Tea or Coffee

Dinner:
Maybe this is a Church
   Dinner Night and you
   can escape cooking. If
   not:
Chicken N' Rice
Steamed Squash
Fresh Green Beans
Salad of your choice
Tea and/or Coffee

Thursday

Breakfast:
Fruit juice
Egg
Bacon
Toast
Coffee

Lunch:
Leftover Chicken N' Rice,
   or
Bologna or other meat
Sandwich
Potato Chips
Onion Wine Soup
Tea or Water

Dinner:
Mexican Casserole
Mexican Salad
Mexican Cornbread
Tea or Beverage of your
   choice

Friday

Breakfast:
2 Alka Seltzer, and/or
Fruit juice
Scrambled Eggs
Toast
Coffee

Lunch:
Leftover Mexican Salad,
    or
Sandwich of your choice,
    or
Soup of your choice
Tea or Water

Dinner:
Crawfish Ettouffée
Rice
Tossed Salad
Tea and/or Coffee

Saturday

Breakfast:
Sleep late, then
Omelet
Coffee

Lunch:
Get all the leftovers out of
    the refrigerator and
    make a stew, or
Surprise Soup
Tea or Coffee

Dinner:
An excellent evening for
    the Uppity Woman to
    take you out to eat. This
    does *not* mean that you
    are not supposed to pay
    for it.

Sunday

Breakfast:
Fruit juice
Toast
Coffee

Lunch:
Eye of Round Roast
Rice
Gravy
Fresh Beans
Tea

Dinner:
The HouseHusband's
  night off!

10

Write Your Own Cookbook

A recipe from the kitchen

of_____

Ingredients:

Step by Step Procedure:

A recipe from the kitchen

of

Ingredients:

Step by Step Procedure:

A recipe from the kitchen

of

Ingredients:

Step by Step Procedure:

A recipe from the kitchen

of

Ingredients:

Step by Step Procedure:

A recipe from the kitchen

of

Ingredients:

Step by Step Procedure:

A recipe from the kitchen

of

Ingredients:

Step by Step Procedure:

A recipe from the kitchen

of

Ingredients:

Step by Step Procedure:

A recipe from the kitchen

of

Ingredients:

Step by Step Procedure:

A recipe from the kitchen

of

Ingredients:

Step by Step Procedure:

A recipe from the kitchen

of

Ingredients:

Step by Step Procedure:

A Cookbook:
Helpful Cooking Hints for HouseHusbands of Uppity Women
E-Heart Press, Inc.
3700 Mockingbird Lane
Dallas, Texas 75205

Please send me_____copies of **A Cookbook: Helpful Cooking Hints
for HouseHusbands of Uppity Women** $12.95

Postage/Handling for 1 book $1.75

Add .50 for each additional book   _____

Texas residents add 8% sales tax   _____

    TOTAL   _____

Send to:_____

Address_____

City_____ State _____ Zip_____

Make checks payable to E-Heart Press, Inc.

A Cookbook:
Helpful Cooking Hints for HouseHusbands of Uppity Women
E-Heart Press, Inc.
3700 Mockingbird Lane
Dallas, Texas 75205

Please send me_____copies of **A Cookbook: Helpful Cooking Hints
for HouseHusbands of Uppity Women** $12.95

Postage/Handling for 1 book $1.75

Add .50 for each additional book   _____

Texas residents add 8% sales tax   _____

    TOTAL   _____

Send to:_____

Address_____

City_____ State _____ Zip_____

Make checks payable to E-Heart Press, Inc.